7 DAYS

FINANCIAL

BREAKTHROU

GH PRAYERS

DANIEL C. OKPARA

Copyright © July 2020 by Daniel C. Okpara.

Published By:

Better Life Media.

BETTER LIFE WORLD OUTREACH CENTER.

Website: www.BetterLifeWorld.org

Email: info@betterlifeworld.org

FOLLOW US ON FACEBOOK

Like our Page on Facebook for updates:

https://facebook.com/betterlifeworld/

This title and others are available for quantity discounts for sale promotions, gifts, and evangelism. Visit our website or email us to get started.

Any scripture quotation in this book is taken from the King James Version or New International Version, except where stated—used by permission.

All texts, calls, letters, testimonies, and inquiries are welcome.

Are you looking for resources to keep your spirit on fire?

Follow me on my Facebook (PRIVATE GROUP) for daily 30-minute morning broadcast. Stir your spirit for Jesus every morning. Start your day with powerful prayers and teachings, and command your breakthrough.

JOIN NOW FOR FREE

www.bit.ly/fb-danielokpara

Table of Contents

Receive Daily and Weekly Prayers

Powerful Prayers Sent to Your Inbox Every Monday

Enter your email address to receive notifications of new posts, prayers and prophetic declarations sent to you by email.

Email Address

Sign Me Up

*Go to: **BreakThroughPrayers** to subscribe to receive FREE WEEKLY PRAYER POINTS, and prophetic declarations sent to you by email.*

www.breakthroughprayers.org

Free Books

Download These 4 Powerful Books Today for FREE...

Take Your Relationship With God to a New Level.

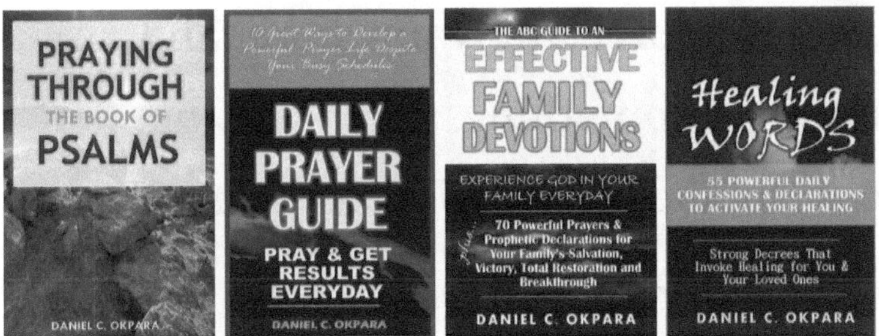

Click Here to Download

www.betterlifeworld.org/grow

HOW TO USE THIS BOOK

Let me start by saying, thank you for downloading this book. I appreciate your time and assure you that something good will happen to your financial situation as you pray with me in this book.

As the title says, pray with this book over seven days.

In the week that we had this program on my FB daily broadcast, the power of God was released in the lives of hundreds of members and listeners. We had great testimonies and divine interventions that produced mysterious connections, open doors, debt cancellations, new jobs, new ideas, and new business startups.

As you read this book, expect strange interventions and miracles. I am praying with you in agreement, and I'm convinced that your story will change. You will encounter God's power that will change your life and move you forward financially.

Here's how I recommend that you pray with this book:

1. Read and finish the first four chapters in the first section and make notes of every thought and inspiration that strikes your heart. Don't rush it. Remember that this is a prayer book. So take your time as you do this.

2. Then declare seven-day fasting to wait on the Lord over your financial situation. This is absolutely very

important. It's part of the heart of this book.

3. The second section is the prayer section. Read one chapter (or prayer day) every day. Ensure to read all scriptures, prayers, and declarations as provided. But as you pray, yield to the Holy Spirit, listen to your heart, and pray beyond the prayer words.

4. I recommend that you pray these prayers in the night, anytime from midnight to 6:00 AM. But if that's not possible, then pray when you can.

5. Pray the prayers in each prayer day, at least three times each of the praying days. Pray before going to bed, wake up in the middle of the

night and pray, and pray in the morning before you start the day.

6. Write down every dream, idea, thought, or direction you receive during prayer and fasting and set out to do them. Remember that all breakthroughs are a product of God's guidance.

I have always taught that we should not stop praying until the mountains move. So, don't stop these prayers after only seven days. The battle against your finances is serious. Come back again and again and use this manual to pray. And don't forget: listen to God's Spirit as you pray. He will show you things you don't know, and suddenly, everything will change.

"As you read this book, expect strange interventions and miracles."

INTRODUCTION

₆Don't worry about anything; instead, pray about everything; tell God your needs, and don't forget to thank him for his answers. ₇If you do this, you will experience God's peace, which is far more wonderful than the human mind can understand. His peace will keep your thoughts and your hearts quiet and at rest as you trust in Christ Jesus. - Philippians 4:6-7 (TLB)

This scripture says that we can and should pray about everything. It says instead of worrying and getting anxious about anything, we should turn those moments of worry into prayers and thanksgiving. If we do, we will experience God's peace beyond human comprehension. His peace will keep our thoughts and our hearts quiet and at rest.

When the Bible says everything, it means everything - your financial needs inclusive. Instead of fearing and fretting about your financial situation, pray about it.

This book is divided into two sections:

Section one contains four chapters and details powerful truths you should know about financial breakthroughs and miracles before starting to pray. The second section comprises seven chapters with powerful short motivations and prayers for financial breakthroughs and miracles.

You will discover compelling insights on financial miracles and breakthroughs, how to pray for financial miracles and breakthroughs, and prayers to command financial miracles and breakthroughs in this book. Then you will confidently pray, and more importantly, you will receive surprising answers to your financial needs.

"Instead of fearing and fretting about your financial situation, pray about it."

SECTION ONE:

UNDERSTANDING FINANCIAL BREAKTHROUGHS AND MIRACLES

Before we start praying, what is financial breakthrough or financial miracles? How do I know God has answered my prayers for a financial breakthrough?

This section covers all there is to know about financial breakthroughs and miracles.

1

WHAT IS FINANCIAL BREAKTHROUGH?

"But my God shall supply all your need according to his riches in glory by Christ Jesus." – Phil. 4:19

There's no central explanation of what *financial breakthrough or miracle* means. It will always depend on individual situations and varied conditions. Depending on who's needing financial breakthrough, it can mean:

- A new or better job

- A raise in salary

- A new business idea

- An improved working condition in the workplace

- An improved relationship with co-workers or supervisors

- Miraculous new business connection

- Divine direction towards an investment decision

- Favor with one's employer

- Favor over one's debts

- Remarkable returns on some investments one was led to do

- Guidance to start a new business

Whatever financial breakthrough or miracle means for you, know that God is not intimidated by any of your problems or needs. He provides and shows us the way of escape in every situation we find ourselves. He will undoubtedly make a way for you as you pray.

PREFER EMPOWERMENT TO HANDOUT

When praying for financial breakthrough or miracle, see it from a holistic perspective. Don't condition your mind expecting a manifestation of quick windfalls to help you solve your financial emergencies. See financial breakthrough and miracles as divine empowerment that enables you to live a life of dominion and lend to others, and not just a manifestation of quick help for your urgent money problems.

What you need is empowerment, not just a handout. And this empowerment can come in diverse ways. Keep your mind open and be expectant that something big will happen. God can send you a handout, but most times, as you will see in other chapters, He'd rather empower you.

Would you rather get a handout or empowerment?

If you're like me, you want both, but want the latter more.

COMMAND SATAN'S ATTACKS TO STOP

Financial breakthrough also means pulling down the strongholds of the enemy over your finances. It also means stopping satan from stealing from you and commanding your lost opportunities to be restored.

Sometimes the devil can attack your finances as he did to that of Job. Nothing scares him more than our prosperity. He knows that if we have financial freedom, we will rapidly stop his works in the lives of people and in many communities and nations.

> **"A prosperous Christian is an instrument of warfare, a big threat to the kingdom of darkness."**

When Pharaoh accepted to let the Israelites leave, he told them to leave their wealth behind (Exodus 10:24). They could go and serve God provided they didn't go with their flocks, gold, and other forms of wealth. Why? He knew that if they were hungry and impoverished, it would only be a matter of time before they voluntarily returned to Egypt.

More people (including millions of youths) have left Church, backslidden from the faith, returned to Egypt, abandoned their calls, and yielded their souls to the devil because of the effect of lack and poverty. We didn't offer them anyway to achieve financial freedom and fulfill their dreams.

Tell yourself the truth: poverty, lack, and inability to provide for your family threatens your faith many times. That daily financial struggles, fights, and questions is not something you celebrate. It distracts many Christians from focusing on God's plans for their lives.

We talk so much about the dangers of the love of money, and that is great. But we also need to talk about the greater dangers of lack and scarcity. We need to strike a balance.

If you are experiencing unusual delays, losses, stagnation, disappointments, or extreme difficulty irrespective of how hard you work and try to make things work, then there may be an attack on your finances. Come in the place of spiritual warfare and stop the works of the devil. Arise and stand on God's Word and rebuke satan over your finances, and command the release of the angels of favor and breakthrough.

DEAL WITH THE 'ASSYRIAN ATTACK'

The devil can build a siege against one's finances. So in seeking financial breakthrough, we must recognize situations that are a result of evil sieges and come against them in warfare.

One thing I always notice in the many financial prayer requests we receive every day is that the prayer requesters constantly say that they are making a lot of effort but not getting rewarded in the degree of their efforts. Sometimes, it seems there is some sort of spiritual chain or burden on their finances. This is usually a result of the work of demons. It is the Assyrian attack.

The devil shivers at a financially empowered Christian, because he knows that money in the hand of a true Christian is an instrument of spiritual warfare and changing of lives. So, he will stop at nothing to keep believers from excelling financially. Let me show you what the Assyrian attack is all about.

And it happened after this that Ben-Hadad king of Syria gathered all his army, and went up and besieged Samaria. And there was a great famine in Samaria, and indeed they besieged it until a donkey's head was sold for eighty shekels of silver, and one-fourth of a kab of dove droppings for five shekels of silver. -

2 Kings 6:24-25

Read that again. Notice that God didn't create that scarcity and problem.

Benhadad, who is a representation of the devil, built a siege on Samaria that led to food prices soaring astronomically. It got so bad that a donkey's head was sold for fifty dollars and a pint of dove's dung for about three dollars. In fact, in 2 Kings 6:28-30, the situation got so terrible that people began to eat their children to survive, all because of the siege built by the enemy.

Here are signs that your finances may be under a siege:

- You're currently going through some severe financial famine;

- You're working so hard, but after all is said and done, there's not much to show for it.

- You desperately want to find a job, and you're doing the best you can, but it's not forthcoming

- Any time a significant financial blessing is coming your way, something just happens, and you lose it.

- When you're due for promotion, you don't get it, even when others who are less qualified get theirs

- You experience extreme disfavor in the workplace; no one wants to help you

- People willfully owe you money and never want to pay, even though they have it

- You can't usually explain how you spend money. You just feel that money comes, but it just runs away

- You're stuck in someplace in life, business, and career. Stagnant and not making any meaningful progress steadily.

- You work for people, and they never want to pay you. You must always struggle to get paid for what you have worked for

- You are always struggling financially

- You have this feeling that something is wrong somewhere.

- You're never out of debt. Before you receive some breakthrough, issues have piled up so much that before the money comes, it's already spent. Thus, you're always forced to continue to struggle.

As we join hands to pray in this book, every Assyrian attack, siege, demon, and barrier against your finances comes to an end, in Jesus name.

"God is not intimidated by any of your problems or needs. He provides and shows us the way of escape in every situation we find ourselves. We just need to pay more attention."

2

GOD AND YOUR FINANCIAL NEEDS

"If you, then, though you are evil, know how to give good gifts to your children, how much more will your Father in heaven give good gifts to those who ask him!" - Matthew 7:11

Looking at me from the opposite side of the table, she sighed, bowed her head, waited a few seconds, then looked up and said, "Pastor, are you sure God is interested in our financial problems?"

I looked at her with compassion. I could see where she was coming from: "If God is concerned about our money problems, why are many believers getting so frustrated financially? Why are Christians struggling so much on money matters?"

About sixty to seventy percent of the prayer requests I receive, both on the counseling table and on our blog center on finance. While the details are different, when summarized, they boil down to money – no money to pay bills, no money to pay rent, no money to start a new business, debtors not wanting to pay, upsetting debts, contract to be approved, money to support health treatment, help for recovery of lost investments, an urgent need for a better job, and so on.

Why is there so much struggle with believers when it comes to money? I can't remember the number of times people have said to me, "But Pastor, I am a faithful tither. I give and sow seeds. But I do not see any breakthrough. What is wrong?"

So, my counselee wanted to know if God is genuinely interested when it comes to money. She had gotten to the point she feels, "Maybe God is just interested in us being spiritual and is not bothered how we survive financially over here."

I knew that my answer would mean a lot to her, so I thought about it carefully. Then a question welled up in my heart, "When your child is in trouble, do you care?"

The scripture says that even though, as humans, we're full of evil thoughts and ways, we care for our children, how much more God, our Father in Heaven? If we humans are worried and concerned when our children are in trouble – whether financially or otherwise – isn't God much more interested, too?

"I sincerely believe that God cares for your financial needs. So, when you're in a financial problem, pray and allow Him to show you a way of escape."

There are many instances of divine intervention in the lives of men and women of God in scriptures to show us that our heavenly Father will always intervene when we call on Him. Let's look at three cases.

THE WIDOW

." The wife of a man from the company of the prophets cried out to Elisha, "Your servant, my husband is dead, and you know that he revered the Lord. But now his creditor is coming to take my two boys as his slaves."

.Elisha replied to her, **"How can I help you? Tell me, what do you have in your house?"** "Your servant has nothing there at all," she said, "except a small jar of olive oil."

.Elisha said, **"Go around and ask all your neighbors for empty jars. Don't ask for just a few. ₄Then go inside and shut the door behind you and your sons. Pour oil into all the jars, and as each is filled, put it to one side."**

.She left him and shut the door behind her and her sons. They brought the jars to her, and she kept pouring.

.When all the jars were full, she said to her son, "Bring me another one." But he replied, "There is not a jar left." Then the oil stopped flowing.

She went and told the man of God, and he said, **"Go, sell the oil and pay your debts. You and your sons can live on what is left."** - 2 Kings 4:1-7

This woman would have lost her two sons to creditors due to the family's debt. She prayed and cried out to Prophet Elisha, who, by the Spirit of God, counseled her on what to do.

We can certainly pray for financial breakthrough. However, praying for financial breakthrough does not mean that money will fall from the sky. This is, perhaps, where our first problem is. We want some unusual sky shaking things to happen as proof that God truly cares and is answering our prayers.

But, in most cases, it doesn't happen that way. So, we wonder, "How is God helping me in this financial distress?"

From my experience, however, what God does is to provide us a way of escape, more like, showing us what to do. Amazingly, this revelation doesn't come in the most unusual, jumping, and shouting manner to make us say, "Yeah, this is God."

Sometimes, God's answers come as a business idea, an offer, or some open door that would require some real extra work. If we're not watchful, we'll trash His answers and continue looking and seeking for some extraordinary reactions.

As soon as this woman prayed, God answered her. But not by canceling the debts. She got an idea that demanded some work. First, she would need to borrow some vessels and reproduce the oil in her house. Then she needed to go out and sell the produced oil.

If you look at it physically, it appears as though there was no special God intervention in the situation. Everything seemed to be the usual, day-by-day approach to business, right?

- Borrow vessels

- Pour the oil inside the vessels

- Go and sell the oil

- Pay your debts

- Live on the balance

Where was the miracle? Where was the special God-factor in all that?

But look at it again. The God factor is there from the very beginning. First, the oil was always in the house. Her husband died, not knowing about it. She began to pray and seek God, and suddenly, the oil became a subject of discussion. That was God's intervention.

> ***"Most times, our means for financial breakthroughs are not too far from us, but we don't see it."***

However, when we start to pray and declare His promises, suddenly, some topics start coming up, and we begin to see things differently – that's God working on things and in us to see.

Secondly, the multiplication of the oil was also a miracle. Think about it. How did one jar of oil suddenly fill so many others if not God? That she put in extra work does not mean God wasn't in the picture. It was she and God working together.

And that's how it works in receiving financial breakthrough. God will show you what to do. This doesn't have to come through a dream, or some unusual, shaky prophetic encounter. It can come through certain discussions of business or a direction coming up, usually after many prayers.

You need to discern what's happening and be willing to explore what you're learning. As you invest your efforts, God multiplies it and ensures you have results far exceeding the ordinary.

Financial breakthrough or miracles is you and God working together, not you waiting in your house while God calls your creditor, calls the supplier, calls the engineer, takes your CV to companies, and carries the goods to go and sell, and returns the cash to you. No, it doesn't work that way.

Like this woman, you may need to put in some extra work to manifest the answer to your financial miracle and breakthrough prayers. Don't be shy about doing what must be done. God can bless you from doing the smallest of all endeavors.

PETER AND HIS COLLEAGUES

One day as Jesus was standing by the Lake of Gennesaret, the people were crowding around him and listening to the word of God.

He saw at the water's edge two boats, left there by the fishermen, who were washing their nets.

He got into one of the boats, the one belonging to Simon, and asked him to put out a little from shore. Then he sat down and taught the people from the boat.

When he had finished speaking, he said to Simon, **"Put out into deep water, and let down the nets for a catch."**

Simon answered, "Master, we've worked hard all night and haven't caught anything. But because you say so, I will let down the nets."

When they had done so, they caught such a large number of fish that their nets began to break. So they signaled their partners in the other boat to come and help them, and they came and filled both boats so full that they began to sink. – Luke 5:1-7

Every fisherman knows that the best time to go fishing is usually in the night because that's when the waters are quiet. That's when you can be sure the fishes, the big ones, will show up and you can have a good business the next day.

Peter and his colleagues knew this and applied the principle in their business. Unfortunately, after the hard labor of the night, they caught nothing.

Sometimes, one can do everything they know how to do, follow all the principles of success they've learned, apply the best skills of the trade, yet experience hardship and setback. I want it to register in your heart that setbacks are not necessarily a proof of something wrong with you or evidence of some spiritual curses against you. It's a normal part of life.

Just like Peter and his colleagues, one may be in a situation where they do not know where the next meal will come from. But as we surrender to God in prayers and listen to His voice, the situation will come under control.

Another thing to learn from this story is to be willing to try again. Even when we have failed over and over, we must be willing and ready to go out to explore again and again. As we try more and more times, not because of what we can see physically, but because we believe God is leading us, we'll see miraculous intervention.

Peter's business frustration turned into a massive harvest of breakthrough when Jesus intervened. As we pray and seek God, expect His intervention that will change the course of events in your career, business, and finances. Miracles will happen.

ISAAC AND THE FAMINE

₁Now there was a famine in the land—besides the previous famine in Abraham's time—and Isaac went to Abimelek king of the Philistines in Gerar.

₂The Lord appeared to Isaac and said, "Do not go down to Egypt; live in the land where I tell you to live.

₃Stay in this land for a while, and I will be with you and will bless you. For to you and your descendants I will give all these lands and will confirm the oath I swore to your father Abraham.

₄I will make your descendants as numerous as the stars in the sky and will give them all these lands, and through your offspring, all nations on earth will be blessed, ₅because Abraham obeyed me and did everything I required of him, keeping my commands, my decrees, and my instructions."

₆So Isaac stayed in Gerar...

[12] Isaac planted crops in that land and the same year reaped a hundredfold because the Lord blessed him.

[13] The man became rich, and his wealth continued to grow until he became very wealthy.

[14] He had so many flocks and herds and servants that the Philistines envied him.

The Bible talks about famine during Isaac's time, besides the famine during His Father, Abraham's time. This means that Abraham and Isaac came to points in their lives they experienced hardship.

Isn't that interesting?

No situation is entirely new. Others have gone through things, sometimes worse things than the ones we are going through. Their examples of victory and deliverance is an encouragement that we will also be delivered and be victorious.

In the case of Isaac, he wanted to travel out of the country, but God instructed him not to. Success does not come from abroad, but from above.

"Hardship is not peculiar to specific countries. It happens in every nation. You can experience it anywhere. So, don't assume that your financial hardship is because of the country you're living in."

Focus on hearing what God wants you to do. That's what is more important.

Following God's voice, Isaac stayed back and planted crops that same year. Putting in extra effort, he and his servants dug wells and found water to water their crops. And God blessed their efforts so much that while others were complaining of the recession and famine, he prospered.

As children of God, we may experience hardship and scarcity. When we do, it doesn't mean God no longer loves us. It doesn't mean we are no longer His children. It doesn't mean the covenant of prosperity is not working for us. Sometimes, hardship and problems are a reminder that we are still in the world. The Bible says that the whole world lies in wickedness.

But there's good news. God has promised that we'll be victorious at all times. So, as we pray, wait, listen, and take inspired steps, we will undoubtedly command supernatural deliverance.

God will deliver you from any type of financial scarcity in your life right now because He cares. If He delivered others before you, He will also deliver you.

May these three stories stir your faith to believe that your financial help prayers are not a waste of time. God will certainly make a way.

"God cares for our financial needs and situations. When we're in financial trouble, we can pray and allow Him to show us a way of escape."

3

MONEY MIRACLES

"Therefore, my people have gone into captivity, because they have no knowledge; their honorable men are famished, and their multitude dried up with thirst. – Isaiah 5:13

A miracle is a divine intervention. Something that alters the normal course of life and produces a positive effect. For instance, the typical way to make money is to render a service or sell a product. Using that definition, one would, therefore, say that a financial miracle is an intervention that helps someone out of a financial situation without directly rendering a service or selling a product.

While that is accurate, it is wrong to peg financial breakthrough and miracle on that premise alone. My experience over the years, both personally and with others, has taught me that's not the best way to look at financial breakthrough or miracle. Unfortunately, for many Christians today, that's how they define and expect a financial miracle.

As a pastor who receives hundreds of complaints and prayer requests every day, may I share with you what I believe a financial breakthrough is not, and what I think it is. This is very important because it will help you to appreciate God's answers as they come. It will help you not to fix your mind in a specific way as the way God must answer your prayers for financial breakthrough.

IT'S NOT WINDFALL MIRACLES

How often have you heard stories like this...

- "After the service, I got a call from so and so person, and he said, 'God told me to send you so and so amount.' And wow, it was precisely the amount we needed. God is great."

- "I gave so and so amount of seed, and the next day, my bank called and said, 'you know what, we're writing off the debt.'"

- "Someone I do not know just called after I sowed a seed and sent us a check of …. thousand dollars."

While these testimonies are real, the challenge is that, over the years, it has made many sincere believers box God's ways of provision into such expectation. When they pray for breakthroughs, what they are often expecting is some sort of strange person calling and blessing them financially.

As a growing Christian, I always wondered why I didn't have such strange miracles, no matter how much I prayed or gave as seeds of faith. I was always wondering why no one ever called me to give me money on God's command, even when I was in desperate need and had sowed seeds of faith. Many times, I thought, "Maybe there are some sins in my life, or some demons from my father's lineage preventing people from seeing visions of me and calling to bless me." A few times, I wondered if God was partial, or that the *tellers* of these testimonies were lying.

It took me years to begin to understand and accept God's impartiality in these testimonies. I started to see things differently. Then, almost like a revelation, I discovered that:

- While these miracles can happen to anyone, they are not the primary way God wants to provide for us financially.

- These types of miracles happen more to pulpit ministers because preaching is their work, and God provides for them through people giving to them.

- If you do not experience such miracles often, it doesn't mean that God loves you less, or that your offerings and seeds of faith are not accepted.

- We cannot live our lives waiting or depending on these kinds of miracles. I call them **windfall miracles**. While God can reach out to us in those ways, most times, to provide relief in severe crises, they are not designed to be the way we live our lives as Christians and believers. Such occasional interventions are not the divine standard for God's provision.

- Our offerings and seeds of faith are accepted whether things happen to us in that manner or not.

I counsel and pray with tens of people daily, and I can tell you that this is still a weighty challenge for most Christians. Dig into their hearts when they pray for a financial breakthrough, you'll discover that, amazingly, what they are expecting is some sort of supernatural windfall. More like money falling from the sky, or someone calling and saying, "God says I should give you fifty thousand dollars," or that they would just wake up and win lotto or win a bet through some strange incidents.

Unfortunately, as I've learned, this is a wrong way to look at financial breakthrough prayers, God's answers and supplies. This ***"Cinderella mindset"*** puts our God into some type of tiny carnal box and limits His ability to bless us financially.

When praying for financial breakthrough, detach yourself from this windfall mindset. Financial breakthrough can come in any (legal) way. You should have an open mind and not confine God to one specific way to answer your prayers. What matters is that He will answer your prayers, but the manner it would take is entirely at His discretion.

Someone said, "So many times we get stuck in a poverty mentality mindset that allows us to believe that the only way we will ever prosper financially is through some handout, or by luck or chance..."

When you sow your seeds and pray for a breakthrough, surrender yourself entirely to God and look up to His doings in your life. Recognize that His thoughts are higher than your thoughts, and His ways than yours. He will answer your prayers. Don't box Him in your small angle or insist He must provide your financial breakthrough by some supernatural money gifts.

Can God send us unsolicited financial windfalls or harvests? Can He touch people to send us money to carry out our projects or solve some urgent financial problems in our lives?

Definitely, yes.

The cattle on a thousand hills are God's (Psalm 50:10). The silver is His, and the gold is His (Haggai 2:8). He can rain down bread from the sky and throw up thousands of fishes from dry land. God is omnipotent, and nothing is impossible with Him.

But we go into error and box God into a corner when we want and insist that He should do something for us in a certain way, instead of discerning what He is already doing in our lives. We go into error when we refuse to accept His methods because it does not align with our expectations.

So, the first prayer you should pray when needing and believing for a financial breakthrough is that God would deliver you from your made-up notions, outright spiritual lies, and comfy, half-truths about money and financial breakthrough.

Sometimes these wrong thinking can become a stronghold deterring us from accessing God's open doors.

IT'S NOT LIVING ON MIRACLE MONIES

Wealth is created by building systems, not by money miracles. Our God will always reach out to us with financial help in times of need, but He wants us to grow and establish systems that don't thrive by needing handouts daily. Look at these scriptures:

Deut. 15: 6 (NLT) - *The LORD, your God, will bless you as he has promised. You will lend money to many nations but will never need to borrow. You will rule many nations, but they will not rule over you.*

Deut. 28:12 (NLT) - *The LORD will send rain at the proper time from his rich treasury in the heavens and will bless all the work you do. You will lend to many nations, but you will never need to borrow from them.*

Genesis 1:26-28 - *26And God said, Let us make man in our image, after our likeness: and let them have dominion over the fish of the sea, and over the fowl of the air, and over the cattle, and over all the earth, and over every creeping thing that creepeth upon the earth.*

27So God created man in his own image, in the image of God created he him; male and female created he them. 28And God blessed them, and God said unto them, Be fruitful, and multiply, and replenish the earth, and subdue it: and have dominion over the fish of the sea, and over the fowl of the air, and over every living thing that moveth upon the earth.

You will not lend to nations or fulfill God's purpose of dominion by living on financial miracles daily. As I said, financial miracles are God's way to give us relief in urgent situations. But after we've received such miracles, we must employ God's resources within us to develop systems that align with His purpose of dominion.

Let me further explain what I mean here with these testimonies:

Case Study 1

A friend's wife delivered a baby through CS. Due to certain complications in the process, the hospital bill was huge. Meanwhile, before this time, this friend was having challenges in his business. So, paying the hospital bill and getting his wife out of the hospital was very difficult.

One day, while in the hospital, bowed and in tears, a man he had never met before, a Muslim (Alhaji) for that matter, walked up to him and asked what the issue was. In tears, he explained his ordeal. The strange man consoled him and paid the hospital bill and gave them some money to go home with.

Now, that's a marvelous divine visitation. Call that man an angel or even God, and you'd be right. It was a great miracle and breakthrough. But as you can see, it will be wrong for this friend to now live his life hoping that an angel will always appear and empower him financially this way.

Case Study 2

When Sis. Blessing joined our Church, she was utterly helpless. A single mom of four children, she needed money every single day to provide food in the house. Unfortunately, she had no visible source of income. And the father of the children did not care. In fact, he had moved on with another woman, leaving Blessing and the children to die or live – whichever they wanted.

Without education or any skill, Blessing was living from hand to mouth. She depended on the goodwill of known and unknown people to survive daily. This was also leading her to make abysmal choices. But how long would she do that?

In helping her, I took it one step after another. First, I encouraged her to want life and believe that tomorrow will be better. It wasn't easy getting her out of depression, but with prayers and constant communication, she started to listen. I placed her on weekly financial support from my personal earning and offered the kids a temporary scholarship so they could, at least, leave the house and go to school every day.

When I saw that she was becoming better after a few months, I moved on to the next step.

"You can't continue like this," I said to her one day. "You have to do something to earn money. You will feel better that way and live happier as well."

It was obvious. She didn't need a prophet to accept that. But the question was, "what would she do?"

I saw that the message resonated with her. She wanted to do something, and was willing to do anything, provided it was legitimate. No matter what people gave her, she needed to earn her own money.

Then we began to pray about it. As we prayed, we also searched. Many times, she came up with different ideas. I didn't agree with some, and some, after she did them a few weeks, they just didn't work. Then one day, while she was going home from church, a policewoman called her and asked, "Do you know how to drive?" "No," she replied. "Then go and learn how to drive," the officer said. There and then, they exchanged numbers.

Three months later, Uju had learned how to drive Auto Rickshaws, popularly called Keke, Keke Maruwa, in Lagos. And by some supernatural intervention, we got one new one for her. Today, she earns her own money doing what she loves and providing and caring for her children as well.

These days, I tease her and say, "Blessing, how is your transport company doing?" She would laugh and reply, "It's doing great, Pastor."

I have seen this model of breakthrough replicated in the lives of many of our members. We teach and almost make it a law in the church that "you must work."

We thank God for supernatural financial supplies and miracles that happen to us when we're in need, but it should not be what we live our lives hoping on and wanting to build our future around.

Case Study 3

A few years ago, I was in a desperate need to pay our house rent. I prayed. I fasted. I sowed seeds. But in the physical, it seemed as though nothing happened.

I didn't wake up one morning and see the need supernaturally go away. My landlady didn't call me and say, "God spoke to me, you should not pay rent this year." In fact, she intensified her demand. She wanted her money paid immediately, or we'll be thrown out of the house. It got so bad that she reported me to different people and said to me one day, "Pastor, if these things you're saying are not working, you can go back to the village."

I felt very humiliated many times. I was praying earnestly. I was confessing positively. I was also giving and sowing, and honestly expected some sort of windfall. But things, instead, got worse.

I had to embark on an emergency journey so that if she called me, I would say, "Ma'am, I'm not in town. I traveled. Please, exercise some patience, when I come back, I'll pay." Unfortunately, I was only escaping the insults and humiliation.

"God, where are you?" I would cry many times.

Till today, I still wonder how we pulled through those days because I didn't get any extraordinary miracle. I guess God did a lot, but because I conditioned my mind, expecting a windfall or a Holy Ghost handout, I did not notice it.

And that's what we do many times. We condition our minds a certain way and believe this is the way God should do it. And if things don't happen that way, we think that God did not answer our prayers.

Unfortunately, we're the ones missing God's answers.

Never forget this: ***God answers your prayers - always. It just may not be as you are expecting them.***

In my case, it was during that season God gave me a great idea that has now transformed many lives and supported many people financially.

Did God answer my prayers? Yes.

Did I get money to pay the rent as I expected? No.

Instead of bills money, God gave me a business idea that required my investment of time and effort. And while I was struggling with my mind and the bills, God began to bless that idea and work.

A financial breakthrough or miracle is not confined to sudden windfalls or lucky breaks. When praying for financial miracles or breakthrough, don't insist on windfalls as the only measurement of God's answer to your prayers.

"A financial breakthrough or miracle is not confined to sudden windfalls or lucky breaks. When praying for financial miracles or breakthrough, don't insist on a windfall as the only measurement of God's answer to your prayers."

4

FUNDAMENTALS OF FINANCIAL MIRACLES OR BREAKTHROUGH

"Anything we set forth to do without God's initial blessing is meaningless. It's important to make sure whatever we do is in the eyes of the Lord, and therefore we ask for his blessing over our work." – Psalm 90:17 (Good News)

There are three fundamentals of financial breakthrough or financial miracle. All supernatural financial interventions and provisions in scriptures follow these fundamentals. Knowing them is important to ready your mind to receive God's answers to your financial breakthrough prayers. They are:

- Divine direction

- Determined effort, and

- Mental innovation

You must understand the role of these essentials to quickly overcome any financial challenge in your life and set yourself on the path to financial dominion.

DIVINE DIRECTION

The main asset for financial breakthrough or miracle is direction. In Genesis Chapter Twenty-Six, there was a famine in the country where Isaac lived. But the same year, God blessed him a hundredfold. He was so prosperous that the citizens of the land became angry and jealous.

> **The man became rich, and his wealth continued to grow until he became very wealthy. He had so many flocks and herds and servants that the Philistines envied him.** – Gen. 26: 13-14

To appreciate the power unleashed in this breakthrough, we must look at the story from the beginning. It is not enough to read those verses and begin to make prophetic declarations with them.

The foundation of this miracle and every other great miracle and breakthrough in scriptures is direction. When the recession started, Isaac wanted to leave the country, but God said to him, "Stay in this land. Don't go nowhere." So, he canceled his travel plans and stayed back. That act of following God's direction was the root of his subsequent breakthrough.

You can succeed anywhere. You can excel, even in the worse hostile environment. What you need is to discern what God is saying and align yourself to His direction.

The Bible says:

> **"If you only obey me, you will have plenty to eat. But if you turn away and refuse to listen, you will be devoured by the sword of your enemies. I, the Lord, have spoken!"** - Isa. 1:19-20 – NLT)

Look at that. It didn't say if you will bring plenty offerings, then you will have plenty to eat. No. It says if you will listen and obey.

The sword of the enemies there does not mean war or death. It suggests scarcity, disappointments, lack, frustration, insufficiency, and all manner of financial challenges. That means, if you don't hear and obey, these things will be rampant around you.

"Genuinely desire and crave for divine direction. That's the first key to any form of breakthrough or miracle."

The many frustrations and endless running up and down that has overtaken many of us today is a result of lack of direction.

As I shared earlier, when I was growing up in the Faith, I was taught that if you needed a financial breakthrough or miracle, sow money seeds. So, I went from place to place, giving and sowing seeds. Unfortunately, I didn't prosper or experience significant financial breakthroughs.

Thank God we survived, but I didn't get the type of financial miracle experiences the preachers said we would have if we only sowed seeds. With time, however, I began to ask myself what was missing. Is it that God lied, or that the preachers didn't tell the whole truth, or that I was the problem?

I eliminated the option of God lying and was left with either the principle is not the complete truth or that I was the problem. And once I began to work on those premises, I started to see things more clearly.

God showed me in scriptures that the key to financial breakthrough and any miracle for that matter is hearing what He is saying and following the instruction per time. In other words, money giving is not all I had to do to experience a financial miracle or turnaround.

"Giving should be a daily lifestyle of every believer. But beyond giving and sowing seeds, we must start to discern what the Lord is saying to us and follow it. Otherwise, we may give everything we have and still not experience any breakthrough."

You are giving and sowing seeds, that's great. Excellent. Continue. But go beyond that. Ask God what He wants you to do and listen attentively in your heart. Every miracle in scripture was a result of someone following an instruction.

This is the formula: Prayer + Giving + Direction + Obedience = Breakthrough.

The widow of Zarephath's flour did not multiply only because she gave, but because she gave in response to God's instruction.

> Then the Lord said to him, "Go and live in the village of Zarephath, near the city of Sidon. There is a widow there who will feed you. **I have given her my instructions.**" - 1 Kings 17:8-9 (TLB)

God had instructed her about feeding Elijah. I believe she prayed about surviving the famine (recession), and God showed her what to do. We don't know how, but we know that God did. It could be through a dream, a trance, an angelic encounter, or whatever. The point is that God had spoken to her, because He said, ***"I have given her my instructions."*** If God said he talked to her, then He did. He's not a liar.

It was not Elijah who told the woman to give her last meal. It was God who had spoken to the woman. Elijah was only confirming what the woman had heard from God.

Yes, the widow argued with Elijah at first because she was human. She wanted some confirmation and assurance that what God had shown her was in order and that she was not losing her mind. When she finally decided to give her last meal as she was instructed, the miracle of multiplication took place.

I can tell you that if I ask two or three widows in our church to give their last meals, that is, to close their accounts and bring all their savings to Church, just as this widow did, they may not experience the multiplication the way it happened to the widow of Zarephath.

Why?

Divine instruction.

They were not instructed, and I was not instructed.

God blesses all giving and financial seeds, but there's a difference when you are instructed and when you're not. If God instructs your heart to give to a person or to a ministry, it's different from just giving randomly to everyone.

Is it wrong to give randomly to every person and to every ministry?

No.

We must do that from time to time. God blesses all giving. But beyond our giving, we must desire, and seek for His instruction in our hearts.

God may ask you to call someone and return his property that you kept without permission, and that would be the key that removes all spiritual barriers to your financial breakthrough. He may say, "Hey! You've forgotten what I told you about tithing. Don't bother about what everyone is saying; just obey me." Or He may tell you to invest in a business or resign from your present job and start another one.

"Don't assume that God's key to your prosperity and breakthrough is only about money giving. It's about giving, direction and obedience."

When there is a business opportunity or job opening before you, don't just rush into it, no matter how posh they look. When things get complicated in your career or business, don't just run away without looking back. Spend time and seek the LORD for direction on what to do.

He may inspire you to go ahead with what you're doing, and that you're only being tempted. Or He may lay it in your heart to explore new doors or just stay away. Direction is the first fundamental key to financial miracle or breakthrough.

DETERMINED EFFORTS

Back to Isaac's breakthrough story. Notice in that story that even though Isaac was walking in obedience, he still didn't prosper automatically. The Bible says he went ahead and planted crops that same year. If you thought that was easy, you need to think again.

First, Isaac had to find a way to get water to water his crops as the famine did not spare him just because he was a child of God, a covenant son. He had to dig wells. At first, the citizens claimed ownership of the wells he and his servants dug. On more than two occasions, he labored so hard to dig wells, and the lazy residents, with their entitlement mentality, chased him away from them.

For many of us today, the first and second time we tried and experience such setback was enough to say, "I think I need some deliverance. I don't think God is in this thing. I need to get out of this town."

But that was not Isaac. He moved on. I am sure he had all kinds of emotions and questions, but what kept him on was that God had said, "Stay in this land." So, he kept on digging wells until the rascals trying to stop him got tired of his persistence.

I asked myself as I looked at this story again: "If God spoke to Isaac, why did he need to work that hard still? I thought because God spoke to him, things would have just moved on smoothly without any obstacle. I felt he would have just sat in his house, and all manner of blessings and supplies would be running to him?"

Now, that's another area we miss it and are tempted to misunderstand God. We assume that if God said we should stay in a place, do something, or start a project, that things would be easy. Unfortunately, that's a wrong assumption.

Things may not be easy because you heard God. At first, it may even look like every devil in hell is unleashed against you. But your victory is certain. You'll come out strong and prosperous.

Don't expect everything to be easy because you're a Christian, or because you fasted and prayed, or because you're sure God inspired you to take the steps you're currently taking. Don't expect everything to come on a platter because you sincerely feel that the job or business you're doing now was a provision from God after prayers.

God didn't promise us an easy life. He promised us a victorious life. Sometimes you might have to dig over and over before the rascals are overcome, and the well becomes yours

So, yes. God inspired your heart to start something after you've prayed, and you're taking steps already. But it's looking hard and challenging. What do you do?

Keep praying, keep pushing, and keep making determined efforts. You will surely breakthrough. Always remember that Isaac planted crops when there was no rain. God didn't say, "Okay, Isaac, I'll send rain to the portion of land where you planted crops." No. Isaac had to dig wells laboriously.

MENTAL INNOVATION

There are so many definitions of the word, innovation. But I like this one:

Innovation means improving something that already exists. It can take the form of creating a new product or be in the form of application of better solutions that meet new requirements, unarticulated needs, or existing market needs.

For me, innovation is continually growing and getting better by the day. Imagine where the world would have been today if we didn't grow past the turbine engines; imagine if our mobile phones remained like it was in the 80s; imagine if we didn't develop transport systems away from camels and oxen.

As believers, we must embrace both personal and workplace innovation. We can't keep doing things in old ways, without improving ourselves, or our systems of service and business, and only depend on prayer and fasting to command our breakthrough.

God spoke to the Israelites and said,

"... Ye have dwelt long enough in this mountain. Turn and resume your journey..." - Deut. 1:6-7.

God was simply saying to them, "You have prayed enough. Arise and make a move towards the promised land."

There is a time to pray, and there is a time to make a move.

Isaac was a covenant son. He prayed. God spoke to him, and he chose to obey. Yet he had to improvise by digging wells. God didn't drill the wells for him. Isaac dug them. That's innovation. He provided a solution to a problem leveraging the technology of his time. While others continued to wait for rain, he was providing them with alternatives and using the same to grow his farm. So why wouldn't he prosper? Why wouldn't he, the same year, become so rich that his host country envied him?

Isaac's prosperity was a combination of:

- Divine direction (obtained in prayer)

- Determined efforts, and

- Mental innovation

"If any people must be creative and innovative in this world, it is believers, because we have the Holy Spirit."

When we receive Christ, the Holy Spirit comes and indwells us. Think about it for a second: This is the same Holy Spirit who moved upon the face of the earth and the waters that had no form and were void, and suddenly form, order, and beauty appeared. This is the same Holy Spirit who is God, living inside us and with us.

We are the people who should never be stranded. We are the ones who should be saving the world with smart, practical solutions, products, and services. Unfortunately, we seem to be the ones always needing help. Why? Because we built ourselves along the lines of waiting for God to do things for us, instead of using His ability in us to change the world.

Today, I challenge you to look at financial breakthroughs, miracles, and prosperity from a holistic perspective. Beyond prayer for immediate handouts, windfalls, and quick help to fix your urgent money problems, desire and demand spiritual empowerment that makes you come up with practical ideas and solutions. We need continual, personal, and workplace innovation to retain financial dominion.

Seek God's direction towards your finance. He will drop new thoughts in your spirit. Then give this path the requisite efforts and innovate around it.

"Your mind is a gift from God designed to bring God's wisdom into the physical realm."

I pray that God will empower you to make relevant and time-sensitive changes in the way you do what you do and remain relevant in God's scheme of things.

SECTION 2:

SEVEN DAYS PRAYERS FOR FINANCIAL BREAKTHROUGH

PRAYER DAY 1: GOD WANTS ME TO PROSPER

"But what saith it, the word is near thee even in thy mouth and in thy heart that is the word of faith which we preach, that if thou shall confess with thy mouth the lord Jesus and shall believe in thy heart that God had raised him up from the dead thou shall be saved, for with the heart man believes on to righteousness and with the mouth confession is made unto salvation." - Rom. 10:8-10

Welcome to Day one of our seven days prayers for financial breakthrough. Today, we're going to internalize God's word about our prosperity and declare it.

I know you've read these scriptures and probably declared them a few times, but we're going to declare them, again and again, today and go to work with them in our minds.

Our first step towards financial breakthrough is to assure ourselves that God wants us to prosper. God is interested in our welfare.

Yes, divine prosperity is not so much about having a million dollars idling away in your account. It's about a life of abundance - abundant health, abundant peace, progress, no lack, and salvation of your soul. You can have all that. Why? Because God wants you to have them.

The thief does not come except to steal, and to kill, and to destroy. I have come that they may have life, and that they may have it more abundantly. - John 10:10

Jesus wants you to have abundant life. Don't look at your troubles and say, "This is not possible. I'm already suffering so much."

Declare God's Word instead and reject the plans of the devil; reject the evil works of darkness and let your mind feed on God's plans for your life.

Today, let's declare these authoritative scriptures repeatedly and allow their message to sink deep into our spirit, soul, and body.

According to our opening scripture, to be saved, you must believe in Jesus Christ; you must also confess with your mouth that Jesus Christ is the Lord and Saviour of your soul. It's a heart and mouth work.

The way we receive Salvation is the same way we must follow to activate and receive His deliverance and promise in any area of our lives. You must believe His promise and declare it. As you do, your spirit accepts it, your soul confirms it, and before you know it, your body will manifest it.

Don't forget that Jesus Christ is the Word. So, when you confess the Word of God, you are also proclaiming Jesus Christ as the Lord and Savior over your health, finances, or the situation you are speaking to. As you do, you invoke His salvation and deliverance.

He sent His word and healed them and delivered them from their destructions. *" - Psalm 107:20.*

Declaring the Word invokes God's healing and deliverance. So let's start the process today.

The confessions below are based on God's promises for your provision and prosperity. Reflect over these scriptures and make the accompanying declarations with authority. Wake up in the middle of the night and read these verses and declare the assertions out loud. Declare them early in the morning, mid-day, evening, and every time you can.

Find other scriptures and add to the examples presented here and go to war with them. The Word of God is the Sword of the Spirit. So, as you release these scriptures from your mouth, you're not just building your faith, you're also releasing spiritual arrows against the forces of darkness working against your abundance and prosperity. You're removing all spiritual and mental obstacles to your prosperity and releasing grace for supernatural intervention and breakthroughs.

#1. GOD WANTS ME TO PROSPER

3 John 1:2 - Beloved, I wish above all things that thou mayest prosper and be in health even as thy soul prospers.

DECLARE:

I am a child of God through Jesus Christ. Today, I remind myself that God wants me to prosper and be in good health, even as my soul prospers.

The Grace that saved me from sin, also established my healing, health, and prosperity.

So, I shall prosper; I shall be in good health, and at the end of all things, I shall be with Jesus in His Kingdom.

#2. GOD DELIGHTS IN MY PROSPERITY

Psalm 35:27 - Let the Lord be magnified, who hath pleasure in the prosperity of His servant.

DECLARE:

God delights in my prosperity, not in my lack, suffering, debt, and beggarliness.

My prosperity, abundance, and success please God.

Today, I declare that in the name of Jesus Christ, I will walk in abundance and prosper in all things I set my hands to do.

#3. I'M A FRUITFUL TREE

Psalm 1:3 - And he (the righteous) shall be like a tree planted by the rivers of water that brings forth his fruit in his season; his leaf also shall not wither, and whatsoever he doeth shall prosper.

DECLARE:

Through my faith in Christ, I am righteous before God.

I, therefore, declare that I am like a tree planted by the riverbank.

I am a well-watered garden.

Henceforth, I will bring forth fruit in season and out of season.

Nothing dies in my hands.

I am a blessing to everyone around me, and whatever I do prosper, in the name of Jesus Christ.

#4. JESUS TOOK MY POVERTY

2 Corinthians 8:9 (NLT) - You know the generous grace of our Lord Jesus Christ. Though he was rich, yet for your sakes, he became poor, so that by his poverty he could make you rich.

DECLARE:

Dear Lord, Jesus Christ, You had it all in Heaven. You created and own the heavens and the earth. You are King in heaven and didn't need a man to enforce Your Kingship.

But for my sake, You came and walked on the earth, choosing to die the death of the poor and sinner, for my deliverance and salvation.

You were rich but chose to be poor for my sake, that I may be rich, and have it all.

I thank You, Lord.

Be glorified today, and forever.

I affirm today that I will not accept anything else other than what God has in store for me through Christ.

I reject poverty, lack, and debt, and I declare that I am rich in salvation, in health, in love, and in money, in Jesus name.

#5. I WILL OBEY AND PROSPER

Job 36:11 - If they obey and serve Him, they shall spend their days in prosperity, and their years in pleasures. (Read also, Deuteronomy 28:1-13)

DECLARE:

Today, in the name of Jesus Christ, I declare that I chose to obey the voice of God. I chose to listen to the Holy Spirit and follow His direction for my career, finances, and business.

Through the Holy Spirit, I access supernatural ideas and insights for financial breakthrough and wealth creation.

The blessings of God are upon me. They will overtake me and cause me to be promoted in all places.

I shall be blessed in the city and blessed in the country.

I shall be blessed in the fruit of my body; the produce of my ground and the increase of my herds shall be blessed; my cattle, business, and investments shall increase beyond man's doing;

The labor of my hands shall be blessed.

My going out and coming in shall be blessed.

God will cause those who rise against me to be defeated before my face; if they come out against me in one way, God will make them to flee before me in seven ways.

The blessing of the Lord is upon my house. I will prosper in the land where I live; every member of my family shall prosper in the land where we are.

The peoples of the earth shall see that we are called by the name of the Lord, and they shall fear God because of me.

God empowers me and my family to abound in spiritual and physical prosperity. We abound in salvation, holiness, soul-winning, properties, money, and generosity, in Jesus name.

#6. I WILL SEEK GOD AND PROSPER

2 Chronicles 26:5 - He sought God in the days of Zechariah, who had understanding in the visions of God; and as long as he sought the Lord, God made him prosper.

2 Chronicles 31:21 - And in every work that he began in the service of the house of God, in the law and in the commandment, to seek his God, he did it with all his heart. So he prospered.

DECLARE:

Going forward, O Lord, baptize me with an unquenchable thirst for righteousness and service in Your Kingdom.

Help me to seek You with all my heart.

As I do, Lord, show me the path to impactful living, and cause me to be a model of Christ's love and compassion.

Cause the works of my hands to prosper and empower me to create wealth.

Through my success, Father, draw others to the love of Jesus Christ, in Jesus name.

#7. I AM NOT FORSAKEN

Psalm 37:25-26 - I have been young, and now am old, yet I have not seen the righteous forsaken, nor his descendants begging bread. He is ever merciful and lends, and his descendants are blessed.

DECLARE:

God is with me.

I am not forsaken.

I am a lender and not a borrower.

I give and receive.

I sow and harvest.

I am not a beggar.

My family and descendants are blessed, in Jesus name.

#8. GOD LOADS ME WITH DAILY BENEFITS

Psalm 68:19 - Blessed be the Lord, who daily loads us with benefits.

DECLARE:

I am connected to the source of all good things.

God is my Father, and I am His child.

Every day, I enjoy His financial abundance, success, and favor, in Jesus name

---

#9. I WILL BE FRUITFUL EVEN IN OLD AGE

Psalm 92:12-15 - The righteous shall flourish like a palm tree; he shall grow like a cedar in Lebanon.

Those who are planted in the house of the Lord shall flourish in the courts of our God. They shall still bear fruit in old age; they shall be fresh and flourishing, to declare that the Lord is upright; He is my rock, and there is no unrighteousness in Him.

DECLARE:

I declare that God is upright, and there is no unrighteousness in him.

God has made me righteous before Him through faith in Christ.

I am planted in the House of God.

I shall flourish in His presence, and I shall bear fruit even in old age

I thrive every day and flourish in all that I do, in Jesus name.

#10. I AND MY HOUSEHOLD SHALL PROSPER

I declare that I fear the Lord, delight in His ways, and chose to follow His instructions.

I declare that my household, my children, and my generation shall be prosperous.

Wealth will never depart from us.

We will be generational givers, lenders, and kingdom influencers.

I declare that from this day forward, me and my household shall never be in darkness.

God's light will shine in all our ways.

We will be generous every day.

Evil shall never come near our dwelling. We will never be afraid of bad news because our trust is in the Lord.

I and my household are bold, confident, and fearless. We triumph over scarcity, lack, and poverty, always.

We triumph over evil men and women and their machinations.

Our influence, prosperity, and generosity are from generation to generation, in Jesus name (Psalm 112:1-9).

#11. I HONOR THE LORD

Proverbs 3:9-10: Honor the Lord with your possessions, and with the firstfruits of all your increase; so your barns will be filled with plenty, and your vats will overflow with new wine.

DECLARE:

I declare today that I am a giver and a sower.

I do not withhold my substance from God because He gifted me all that I have, and all I will ever have will come from Him.

I, therefore, chose to honor the Lord with my money, with my offerings, with my seeds of faith, and with my possessions.

I reject every form of greed and stinginess henceforth. God owns all and can instruct me to give at any time.

As I honor the Lord, abundance will be in my home. My harvest and barns shall be greatly increased, and my vats filled with new and precious wine.

#12. I AM GENEROUS

Proverbs 11:25: The generous soul will be made rich, and he who waters will also be watered himself.

Proverbs 28:27: He who gives to the poor will not lack, but he who hides his eyes will have many curses.

Isaiah 58:10-11 - If you extend your soul to the hungry and satisfy the afflicted soul, then your light shall dawn in the darkness, and your darkness shall be as the noonday.

The Lord will guide you continually, and satisfy your soul in drought, and strengthen your bones; you shall be like a watered garden, and like a spring of water, whose waters do not fail.

DECLARE:

I am a generous soul.

I water others and support others to grow.

Therefore, I shall be rich.

God will always guide me.

I shall never live in lack and scarcity

I shall be watered when I need to be watered.

And God will always touch kings to provide for my needs, in Jesus name.

#13. MONEY WILL SERVE ME

"I reject the god called mammon.

I reject greed and love of money in my heart.

I ask God for mercy in every area of my life that I have exhibited greed, self-indulgence, and insatiability.

I receive grace for contentment while I seek to reach greater heights in God's purpose for my life.

Money is meant to serve me and not me to serve it.

I will not put money ahead of integrity, no matter what.

As I seek and serve God, He will continue to supply all my needs, in Jesus name."

(Matthew 6:24, 1 Timothy 6:10, Hebrews 13:5)

#14. GOD WILL SUPPLY MY NEEDS

God will supply my needs according to His riches in glory in Jesus Christ, not according to my bank balance.

I, therefore, renew my trust in God and decree that I am not afraid of anything.

As the following needs below are staring at me right now…

(mention those specific needs),

…I confess that I am confident that God is in control and will meet these needs on time, in Jesus name" (Philippians 4:19)

#15. I AM ABOUNDING IN GOOD WORKS

The real purpose of money and God's provisions is for me to abound in good works.

I am created to be a blessing to others.

God is able to make all grace abound to me, so that having all sufficiency in all things at all times, I may abound in every good work, in Jesus name." (2 Cor. 9:8)

#16. IF GOD CARES FOR BIRDS, CERTAINLY, HE CARES FOR ME

The birds of the air do not sow nor reap nor gather into barns. They do not have bank accounts; they do not save, invest, buy, and sell.

Yet God feeds them and takes care of them. And I am more valuable than them.

If God does take care of these birds and other animals that do not even work, I am very confident that He will always take care of my family and me, and in all situations, in Jesus name." (Matthew 6:26)

#17. I REFUSE TO WORRY ABOUT MONEY

From today, I declare that I am not going to be like the people of the world who worry and fight for money, houses, clothes, food, properties, and other stuff.

I am a child of God through Christ Jesus.

I am saved and going to heaven.

While I live in this world, God knows all my needs. He gives me business ideas, money-making strategies, and gives me even the wealth of the heathen.

God teaches me how to do business and profit.

He knows all my needs, and He will provide for me as I continue to serve Him, put Him first in my life, and strive daily to live as He wants me to, in Jesus name."

(Matt. 6:31-32)

#18. GOD IS LEADING ME TO MY GREEN PASTURES

Through the Holy Spirit, the Lord is my Shepherd; He is providing everything I need!

As His sheep, He is leading me and bringing me to green pastures where I will lay down in abundance.

He leads me beside the quiet waters and renews my strength every day.

He empowers me to live and walk in righteousness and do what pleases Him daily.

Even when I'm going through very tough times, I will not let fear rule my heart, for God is with me. He is protecting and guiding me all through the situation.

God is preparing a table for me, and I will enjoy, even in the presence of my enemies.

He is anointing my head with oil, and my cup will run over.

God's goodness and unfailing kindness shall be with me all of my life, and afterward, I will live with Him forever in heaven, in Jesus name." – (Psalm 23:1-6)

#19. I WILL REMAIN THANKFUL

Once again, I declare that I will not be anxious about anything.

Yes, sometimes, my heart may be afraid, and the situation before me may look hopeless and critical.

But, in everything, I reject fear and worry.

I am thankful to God in all, and I'm convinced that He will never leave me nor forsake me. His plans for me are plans for peace and not of evil.

*It doesn't matter what's happening today;
I am very very confident that God is
bringing me to the future He plans for me,
a great and prosperous one, in the name
of Jesus Christ.* (Jer. 29:11, Phil. 4:6)

#20. MY SEEDS OF FAITH AND RIGHTEOUSNESS WILL PRODUCE

Heavenly Father,

*I have sown seeds many times, as You
provided for me.*

*I acknowledge, Lord, that there have been
times when I gave with a wrong mindset,
and even planted in places that were not
good grounds.*

*In those times, Lord, I ask for Your mercy
and forgiveness.*

O Lord, You are the One who supplies seed to the sower and bread for food to the eater.

I pray, Lord, multiply my seeds, and increase the harvest of my righteousness in Christ Jesus.

Enrich me in every way so that I will be generous in every way and produce thanksgiving to You at all times, in Jesus name." (2 Cor. 9:8-11)

#21. GOD IS A GOOD FATHER

Physical parents, though human and full of evil, desires good things for their children and provide for them according to their power. How much more God, our heavenly Father.

I decree today that as I ask, seek, and knock, I shall receive, I shall find, and the door shall be opened unto me.

I will receive all the good things that I desire and have asked of the Lord.

From today, I will not be embarrassed or be put to shame because of money, for God owns all the money on this earth, in the name of Jesus Christ." (Matthew 7:7-11)

#22. I WILL NOT LABOR IN VAIN

"I shall eat the labor of my hands, and it shall be well with me, in Jesus name"
(Psalms 128:2)

#23. I HAVE THE POWER TO CREATE WEALTH

Wealth creation is part of the covenant.

I am a seed of Abraham through Jesus Christ. I am connected to his blessing.

God has empowered me to create wealth.

It doesn't matter where I am today; I am creating generational wealth.

I am an employer of labor, in Jesus name." – (Deut. 8:18)

#24. AS I DECREE, SO SHALL IT BE

Today, in the name of Jesus Christ...

I command money to come to me from the east, west, north, and south.

I break every curse of servitude in my life.

I decree that I will no longer labor in vain.

God restores my dignity, supernaturally.

I declare that the things that men struggle for are coming to me by God's power, in strange ways; they are coming to me with ease.

I decree supernatural intervention over every need in my life right now.

I declare that my past seeds of faith are turned into a supernatural harvest for me.

I decree that the doors of abundance, the doors of prosperity, and the doors of wealth are open unto me.

I decree that I will no longer be embarrassed because of money; I will no longer be insulted because of money.

Every phone call that I made and was rejected, I decree that as I make these calls again, I will be accepted.

I command every evil covenant, every evil curse, every evil statement, and every generational stronghold standing in my life, standing between me and my financial breakthrough to be destroyed today, by the blood of Jesus Christ.

Thank You, Jesus.

It is my season of abundance.

It is my season of breakthrough.

My hands are blessed,

My life is blessed,

My mind is blessed,

My health is blessed,

Everything about me is blessed in the name of Jesus.

Amen.

"As I serve God, I access the path to impactful living. I am and will continue to be a model of Christ's love and compassion. I have knowledge and power from above to create wealth.

Whatever I touch is blessed, in Jesus name"

PRAYER DAY 2: DIVINE DIRECTION

₁₂Then Isaac sowed in that land, and received in the same year a hundredfold: and the Lord blessed him. ₁₃And the man waxed great, and went forward, and grew until he became very great: ₁₄For he had possession of flocks, and possession of herds, and great store of servants: and the Philistines envied him. – Gen. 26:12-14

In the opening verses of Genesis 26, the Bible said, ***"Once again a famine spread through the land***

similar to the one that occurred in Abraham's time."

Whether you call it famine, economic recession, hardship, lay off, or pandemic, it is the same thing. It was a time of crisis.

Today, there is so much negative news and sometimes, visible, real, threats of global recession and crisis. Many are being laid off their jobs, and many more will be laid off. The situation of things in our world are going to get worse.

How should we respond to a national crisis, global problem, or even unexpected personal financial issues like loss of a job, low sales, reduced, low or no income? What should you do if you suddenly find yourself surrounded by needs with little or no resources to handle them? How do you respond?

Isaac's experience gives us an exact victory and breakthrough method to copy during economic hardship. His experience shows us what to do.

> ***...So Isaac went to the town of Gerar, to King Abimelech of the Philistines. The Lord spoke to Isaac and said, "Don't go down to Egypt. Live in the land that I commanded you to live in (Gen. 26:1-2)***

The first thing we do when our finances, jobs, or businesses are affected is wanting to handle situations in the flesh. We start looking for who to borrow money from, start looking for other jobs, or start complaining from place to place. But that's not always the right things to do.

Seek the face of God for divine direction. That was the first key to Isaac's breakthrough and success during the national economic crisis.

. ₂The Lord spoke to Isaac and said, "Don't go down to Egypt. Live in the land that I commanded you to live in… ₆So Isaac settled in Gerar. (Gen. 26:1-26)

Isaac heard God's voice and obeyed. Afterward, he planted crops, and despite the hardship, he reaped a hundredfold that same year.

Let's come before God today and pray for direction. Use the following declarations and prayers to build your faith to receive

God's guidance as you wait on Him. Internalize these Scripture-based prayers and confessions as you seek His instruction and direction regarding your financial breakthrough.

THE PATH TO TAKE

Proverbs 3: 6 - Seek his will in all you do, and he will show you which path to take.

Psalm 16:11 - You will show me the path of life; in Your presence is fullness of joy; at Your right hand are pleasures forevermore.

DECLARE:

God will show me profound mysteries beyond man's understanding because he knows all hidden things. He is light, and darkness does not stop him. He will show me His secret and cause me to walk in His path.

As I seek His will regarding my finances, career, and business, He will show me what to do.

In His will are pleasures and abundance. That is my desire and reality.

I will live in His presence and be joyful forever and ever.

HE IS MY SHEPHERD

Psalm 23: 1 - The Lord is my shepherd; I shall not want.

DECLARE:

The Lord is my Shepherd; He leads me, guides me, and protects me.

I shall not be in lack.

Every day, God, through the Holy Spirit and mysterious circumstances, will lead me into the path of peace and prosperity, in Jesus name.

I WILL RECEIVE CLEAR INSTRUCTION

Psalm 32:8-9 - The Lord says, "I will guide you along the best pathway for your life. I will advise you and watch over you. Do not be like a senseless horse or mule that needs a bit and bridle to keep it under control."

DECLARE:

God will instruct me and lead me in the way I should go. He will guide me with His eyes.

As I think and pray about my finances, business, and job, God will lead me in the way to go.

I will never be confused.

I am not like a horse or mule that must be beaten with whips before they know what to do.

I am a Holy Spirit-filled child of God.

My mind receives unambiguous instructions henceforth, in Jesus name.

I KNOW WHAT TO DO

Psalm 119:104-105 - [104] Through thy precepts I get understanding: therefore, I hate every false way. [105] Thy word is a lamp unto my feet and a light unto my path.

DECLARE

The LORD is ordering my steps every day.

As I read the Word, I will find the light on what to do

As I listen to inspired messages, I will receive illumination concerning my business, career, and finances, because His Word is a lamp to my feet and a light to my path, in Jesus name.

I WILL HEAR AND UNDERSTAND

Isaiah 30:21 - And thine ears shall hear a word behind thee, saying, this is the way, walk ye in it, when ye turn to the right hand, and when ye turn to the left.

DECLARE:

I trust God with all my heart; I do not lean on my own understanding.

As I acknowledge God in all my ways, He will direct my paths.

He will speak to me the way I will understand, and I will walk in His way, whether I turn to the right or to the left.

I WILL NOT WALK IN DARKNESS

John 8:12 - Then spake Jesus again unto them, saying, I am the light of the world: he that followeth me shall not walk in darkness, but shall have the light of life.

DECLARE:

Because I continuously desire to do God's will, I shall know when something is from God or not.

I am following Jesus every day, so I shall not walk in darkness, in Jesus name.

THE HOLY SPIRIT SHOWS ME THINGS

John 10: 13 - Howbeit when he, the Spirit of truth, is come, he will guide you into all truth: for he shall not speak of himself; but whatsoever he shall hear, that shall he speak: and he will shew you things to come.

DECLARE:

When God speaks to me, I will know.

I will not miss His voice, and I will not respond to strange voices.

The Holy Spirit is the Spirit of Truth.

He is in me and is guiding me into all truth.

He will tell me things to come.

He will show me the right course of action in my business, career, ministry, and calling.

He will show me, every day, how to make profit and excel in the works of my hands, in the name of Jesus Christ.

PRAYERS

Philippians 2:13: For it is God which worketh in you both to will and to do of his good pleasure.

Dear Heavenly Father,

I surrender my desires to You from now onwards.

Work in me to desire and pursue only those things that align with Your plans for my life.

Help me to chose investments, businesses, careers, and jobs that are in line with Your grand purpose for my life.

Deliver me from my own plans, which may seem reasonable in my eyes but are the ways of death.

Cause me to recognize Your peace, which is a signal of progress, or Your internal struggle (inside of me), which is a sign of retreat, in Jesus name.

Father, I pray today, if there is any instruction, direction, or guidance that I have ignored in the past, knowingly or unknowingly, which is now responsible for my being spoiled, plundered, and trapped in financial setback, Father, I ask for Your mercy.

O Lord, forgive and restore whatever the enemy has tinkered with in my life, family, and destiny, as a result of not listening to

Your instructions and not following your guidance in the past, in Jesus name.

Father, I pray for spiritual restoration, health restoration, and financial restoration.

O Lord, remove any persistent grudge buried in my heart against anyone; free me from every form of unforgiveness, enmity, and every other thing blocking my spiritual vision and spiritual hearing, in the name of Jesus Christ.

Heavenly Father,

I pray today that every idol of personal opinions and conceptions present in my heart, consciously or unconsciously, be melted away by the fire of the Holy Spirit.

Give me the spirit of revelation and wisdom in the knowledge of You.

Teach and show me the next steps to take about my finances, in Jesus name.

Father, through the Holy Spirit, remind me what You said to me in the past that I ignored or unknowingly walked away from.

Teach me how to receive answers to my financial breakthrough prayers and desires.

Teach me how to make profit, how to live debt-free, and how to create wealth, in Jesus name.

I declare that, in the name of Jesus Christ...

I am walking into my green pastures from today.

I declare that I trust God with all my heart and do not lean on my own understanding.

I acknowledge You, Lord, over my finances, business, career, and all money-related pursuits.

Help me, Lord, to walk in integrity and follow ideas and thoughts that stem from You alone, in Jesus name.

Father, remember You said that if anyone lacks wisdom, let him ask, and You will give him.

Father, I lack the wisdom to proceed financially; I lack the wisdom of specific things to do to move forward financially.

Today, O Lord, I ask You for wisdom and insight that will empower me to walk into financial abundance, in Jesus name.

I decree and declare that:

God cares for me.

He wants it to be well with me.

He did not spare His only begotten Son, but delivered Him up for us, how will he not freely give us all other things?

Satan, this day, I bind you; I command all your attacks and projections against my finances to be destroyed, in Jesus name.

I untie my finances from the hold of the devil, and decree extra-ordinary supplies to come to my possession from this day forward, in the name of Jesus Christ.

Today, O Lord, I command to be destroyed whatever the devil has done in my mind and in my life, causing me to be spiritually blind and unable to access ideas and revelations from You, in Jesus name.

I command every evil oppression and attack on my mind, my dreams, and my visions to cease from today.

I reject all lies, assumptions, and strongholds from the devil about my finances, from today, in Jesus name.

I declare today that...

God is ordering my steps;

He is showing me what to do regarding my finances;

I am getting connected to everyone that is connected to my breakthrough.

I am receiving the right jobs, the right offers, the right business open doors, the right investments and savings plans, and the right money-making opportunities, in the name of Jesus Christ.

From now onwards, I declare that I am connected to the right people that God has ordained for my financial help and breakthrough, in Jesus name.

Today, O Lord, I pray:

When I lay down to sleep, may my dreams bring me clarity about Your direction;

When I am discussing with people, may my discussions bring me clarity;

When I am are thinking of what to do, may my thoughts bring me clarity;

May there be no more confusion in my mind henceforth, in the name of Jesus Christ.

I no longer accept confusion of mind in the name of Jesus Christ.

Father,

I thank You, and give You praise for directing and guiding me over my finances.

I thank You, Lord, that I am walking in a clear direction.

Just like Isaac, I know what to do, where to stay, what to plant, and how to plant, in Jesus name.

Amen.

PRAYER DAY 3: FAVOR

And so God's blessings are not given just because someone decides to have them or works hard to get them. They are given because God takes pity on those he wants to. – Romans 9:16

In literal terms, favor means special treatment or preferring someone over another. In scripture, favor is receiving spiritual and physical benefits that one would not have received from the standpoint of efforts or work. When the Bible says that "the horse is ready for battle, but victory belongs to God," and "it is not of him that willeth, nor of him that runneth, but of the Lord who showeth mercy," it is simply talking about favor.

Favor doesn't mean receiving freebies without work. No. Favor also works with work. However, favor is that extraordinary backing, preference, and exceptional, often undeserved, backing that makes work look outstanding and fabulous.

Hard work is excellent. But you also need favor.

There are heights in life that hard work cannot take you. There are situations that you need favor to deal with, and there are doors that only favor is what will grant you access.

Today's reading says that blessings are not given just because someone wants them.

They are given because God takes pity; that is, because God shows favor.

Favor is one of the mysteries in the Bible that we may not understand its sagacity. However, rather than question its veracity, submit to God and desire favor every day.

Favor is a mystery that God uses to establish His purpose on the earth. Sometimes it may seem unfair in our carnal estimation, but it is what it is. God ordained favor as a tool for bringing His purpose to pass.

> *"At a point in your life, you will need favor to make headway."*

Favor can make a difference in everything you do. Favor can take you to where your talents cannot take you.

When favor speaks for a person, even their enemies cannot but be a blessing to them.

When favor is on your life, even when people don't like you, you will be sitting on a table before them.

God says He prepares a table before us in the presence of our enemies. That's mysterious. But that's favor.

Favor is a fascinating mystery designed by God to enforce the restoration of lost years. Declare the favor of God over your life, over your family, and over the works of your hands every morning. You will begin to command mysterious interventions in your life that will empower you to recover all your years of setback.

HOW TO ACCESS GOD'S FAVOR

There are four ways to activate divine favor in your life. They are desire, prayer, preparation and proper utilization of opportunities

1. DESIRE

I once knelt to pray in the property of one of the most successful ministries in the world. Immediately I knelt, I heard a voice in my heart say, "Whatever anyone has done, anyone can do it. It is subject to desire and hard work."

Napoleon Hill said that "Desire is the starting point of all achievement, not a hope, not a wish, but a keen pulsating desire which transcends everything."

What you don't desire you can't command.

To activate favor in your life, desire favor. The Scripture says, "Therefore I say unto you, what things soever ye desire, when ye pray, believe that ye receive them, and ye shall have them" (Mark 11:24).

2. PRAYER

Someone said, "To burn with desire and keep quiet about it is the greatest punishment we can bring on ourselves."

Once we genuinely desire change and breakthrough in our lives, one of the things we can do is to pray.

> **"Jabez prayed to the God of Israel and said, "I pray that you would bless me and give me more land! Be near me, and don't let anyone hurt me! Then I will not have any pain."**

God gave Jabez what he asked for (2 Chro. 4:10 -ERV).

Prayer is a powerful key for commanding favor in life. The thing about asking is that we always receive. So don't sit and hope that things will take a better shape with time. While waiting, engage the force of prayer and demand favor in the works of your hand. Declare it every morning: "I have favor with God and with man."

3. PREPARATION/VALUE

"... The virgin's name was Mary, the angel went to her and said Greetings, you are highly favored. The Lord is with you." – Luke 1:27-28

Mary's choice for the birth of the Messiah was an act of divine favor. It's favor because she was not the only virgin in

Israel. But there's the work part also. She had to be a virgin to be chosen. She had to prepare herself beforehand. That's what I call the law of value or preparation.

Mary kept herself pure, and when the opportunity came, favor located her. Favor does not mean you should sleep and do nothing, and one day, you'll wake up and see yourself blessed and prosperous. No, it doesn't work that way. You need to prepare yourself. You need to become a person with value to give. Your physical preparation is vital in the supernatural system of favor.

4. DON'T MISUSE OPPORTUNITIES

I once contracted a young furniture maker, who is the choir leader in his church, for an upholstery remodeling job. He told me the job would be ready in three weeks. Because of his position in his church, I intended to make him a long-term supplier for my other projects and that of the Church. I sincerely wanted to encourage him with jobs and recommendations.

Unfortunately, three weeks came and passed, nothing. It took a lot of calls, begging, and all sorts of exchanges for the job to be ready after about two months. And when the job was finally delivered, it was a poorly done work. Everyone saw that the job was done in haste and without any touch of professionalism. To say that I was disappointed in what he did was an understatement. He didn't need prayers to know that was the last contract he was getting from me.

Nothing closes the door of favor as misusing opportunities. Many believers fast and pray for favor but mishandle opportunities and open doors when they come. Yet they wonder why more doors aren't opening for them.

The thing about doors is that open doors always leads to other open doors. So be careful how you treat the little breakthroughs and blessings that God sends your way. The Bible says,

₁₀Whoever can be trusted with small things can also be trusted with big things. Whoever is dishonest in little things will be dishonest in big things too. ₁₁If you cannot be trusted with worldly riches, you will not be trusted with the true riches. ₁₂And if you cannot be trusted with the things that belong to someone else, you will not be given anything of your own. – Luke 16:10-12

PRAYERS

For thou, Lord, wilt bless the righteous; with favor wilt thou compass him as with a shield (Psalm 5:12)

.....

O Lord, encompass me with Your favor like a shield.

Cause me to be at the right place and at the right time, in Jesus name

---

Every attack of men and women, humans or spirits, against my finances, against my life, against my marriage, be canceled today, in the name of Jesus Christ.

Today, I decree and declare that...I have favor with God.

I will find favor with men and women.

I will find favor with kings and princes

I will find favor with my spouse

I will find favor with everyone I meet henceforth, in the name of Jesus.

I declare that God will arise and have mercy on me, for the time to favor me has come; yeah, this is my time of favor (Psalm 102:13).

I declare that by God's favor...

I receive answers to every prayer I have made in the past.

And I receive a supernatural harvest for every seed I have sown in the past, in the name of Jesus.

The Bible says that *Joseph found favor in Potiphar's eyes and became his attendant. Potiphar put him in charge of his household, and he entrusted him to his care, everything he owned.*

I declare today, Lord,

Wherever I work and do business, I have favor with people.

I find favor in my place of work.

I am celebrated in my ministry and place of divine assignment, in Jesus name.

In the name of Jesus Christ, I decree that I find favor with anyone connected to my financial breakthrough.

When God wants to help a man, He sends a man.

Sometimes, our helpers are around, but because our eyes are blinded, we are not seeing them.

Father, Lord, open my eyes to recognize and be connected to anyone You have sent to be a blessing to my life and destiny.

And may the eyes of anyone supernaturally designed to be a helper to my destiny and life be opened to recognize their assignment in my life, in Jesus name.

As God was with Joseph, He is with me. He has not changed. He is the same yesterday, today and forevermore.

I, therefore, declare that I am finding favor with my bosses, supervisors, colleagues, and clients, in the name of Jesus Christ.

Today, I banish the spirit of hatred, curses, and offensive jealousy and envy against me, in the mighty name of Jesus Christ.

From today,

I decree that God is fighting my battles.

I am a victor and not a victim.

I am going forward, from glory to glory.

Whatever I lay my hands upon and whatever I touch will prosper, for God says that I am like a tree planted by the sides of the river, in Jesus name.

I decree that...

I have favor with kings in high places.

I have favor with everyone I work and do business with.

I have favor with the government, in the name of Jesus.

God's favor is at work in my life, henceforth.

I, therefore, command that every contract I have applied for, every tender I have made, wherever my CV is, in the name of Jesus Christ, may they receive special attention and be approved, in Jesus name.

I decree that I am not lazy.

I am not idle and will never be idle

I am a person of value.

I have exceptional skills and the tongue of the learned.

I make things happen

Therefore, I will stand before kings and princes;

I will offer my services before great people, and not before mean and ordinary people, in Jesus name.

God is blessing me with favor and honor. No good thing will He withhold from me. With Him, I am a majority.

From today,

I receive grace to do everything God has called me to do.

Whatever attitude that the enemy has planted in me that is making me not to excel in favor, let it be uprooted in Jesus name.

I receive grace to carry out every business idea God is giving me and to execute my job with the excellency of wisdom from above, in Jesus name.

From this day forward...

Favor will speak for me in the morning, in the afternoon, in the evening, and all the days of my life, in the name of Jesus Christ.

I decree that I will no longer remain at one spot; I will no longer stay stagnant.

I curse the spirit of delay and stagnation, and I cast them into the abyss.

I receive divine touch that accelerates my efforts and commands speedy results in the works of my hands, in the name of Jesus Christ.

Every wrong person stationed in my life, preventing the right persons from showing up, in the name of Jesus Christ, I chase them away.

From today, I begin to attract the right people into my life and destiny.

I begin to attract the right connections, and breakthroughs, in Jesus name.

In the name of Jesus Christ, I declare that...

I have the spirit of creativity.

I create and invent things.

I provide smart solutions to problems.

I find ways where others are stuck.

Light is continually shining in my ways, and people are learning how to do things from me.

Thank You, Jesus, for answered prayers.

Thank You for causing everyone and everything to work for my good and the good of my finances.

Thank You for causing people to want to help and support me in the works of my hand.

Thank you for blessing me with the spirit of creativity.

Thank You for causing me to make the right decisions at all times, in Jesus name, I pray.

Amen.

"Favor is a mystery that God uses to establish His purpose on the earth. Sometimes it may seem unfair in our carnal estimation, but it is what it is. God ordained favor as a tool for bringing His purpose to pass."

PRAYER DAY 4: UNCOMMON WISDOM

24*On their arrival in Capernaum, the collectors of the Temple tax[e] came to Peter and asked him, "Doesn't your teacher pay the temple tax?"*

25*"Yes, he does," Peter replied. Then he went into the house. But before he had a chance to speak, Jesus asked him, "What do you think, Peter? Do kings tax their own people or the people they have conquered?"*

26*"They tax the people they have conquered," Peter replied. "Well, then," Jesus said, "the citizens are free! 27However, we don't want to*

offend them, so go down to the lake and throw in a line. Open the mouth of the first fish you catch, and you will find a large silver coin. Take it and pay the tax for both of us." - Matthew 17:24-27

This is an amazing story. When I studied it recently, the Lord began to open my eyes to the mysteries of supernatural wisdom and insight. As I've said over and over in this book, financial breakthrough means different things to different people. For some, financial breakthrough implies the ability to pay off their debt. For some, it means the ability to settle the mortgage. For some, it means a new job or a new business idea. It can also mean favor in the workplace.

But whatever your definition or understanding of financial breakthrough is, please add this one:

"*Financial breakthrough is the wisdom to know what to do at every point in time. It is having the unusual intelligence that prevents you from being stuck.*"

Now, look at the story we read above. Jesus came to a point that he was about to be embarrassed because of money. But by some strange insight, He knew where to go for the exact amount He needed at that time.

I asked myself a few questions while reading this scripture. I said inside me:

"Jesus, were you in Your capacity as God in this instance, or You were still in Your capacity as a man filled with the Holy Spirit?"

And the Spirit of God said in my heart, "Jesus was in His capacity as a man filled with the Holy Spirit."

Through the Holy Spirit, He had access to God's wisdom that enabled Him to know exactly what to do, exactly where to go, and exactly who to meet. And as a result, the enemy's planned embarrassment was thwarted.

Now, that's what I call living in breakthrough - having access to uncommon wisdom that teaches you what to do, shows you where to go, and who to meet at every point in your life, and prevents you from being stuck and embarrassed.

Compare this story with Jacob's experience in Genesis chapters 30 and 31. Jacob demanded his freedom after serving for twenty years. His master, Laban, tried to trick and defraud him. Leaving his master without full compensation for his efforts would mean frustration along the way.

However, God gave Jacob wisdom that taught him what to do. And even though this was a time that there was little or no veterinary training, biological science, genetics, or whatever, he created a solution that multiplied his assets and saved his empire.

How did Jacob devise such a brilliant system that put him ahead and prevented him from being embarrassed by his cunning boss? By some mystery, he employed strange genetic breeding rules to take back what was stolen from him, how did he do that? The simple answer is supernatural wisdom from God.

There is a wisdom that prevents you from being stuck at any point. This wisdom also empowers you to command double for your trouble. It is wisdom from above. Let us ask God for this wisdom today.

PRAYERS

The Bible says in 1 Corinthians 10:13 that there is no temptation we face that is not common to others. And God is faithful; He will not allow us to face temptations that are beyond our capacity to handle. He will also make a way of escape for us.

I, therefore, pray today, Lord, show me the way of escape from every financial situation in my life right now, in the name of Jesus Christ

---

Heavenly Father, baptize me with Your way of thinking, with Your way of speaking, and with Your wisdom, in Jesus name.

By the Holy Spirit, I access every supernatural way of escape that God has opened for me, in Jesus name.

The Scripture says in the book of 2 Timothy 1:7 that God has not given us the spirit of fear but of love, of power, and of a sound mind.

I, therefore, decree, in the name of Jesus Christ...

I have a sound mind.

I think creatively.

And I solve problems supernaturally.

From today, I erase every form of confusion in my mind by the blood of

Jesus Christ. And I reject the spirit of fear, in the name of Jesus Christ.

I have the mind and the tongue of the learned.

I know what to do, and I know what to say at every given point in time.

I know what to say to my seniors

I know what to say to my neighbors.

I know what to say to my colleagues,

I know what to say to my clients,

For God has given me the tongue of the learned, in the name of Jesus Christ.

The light of God shines on in my mind.

There is no darkness or shadow anymore.

And there is no confusion from this day forward, in the name of Jesus Christ.

In the morning, O Lord, instruct my heart with knowledge. And in the night, teach me supernatural ways that empower me to be a blessing to my generation in the name of Jesus Christ.

The Bible says in 2 Corinthians 10:3-5, "Even though we are humans, we do not wage war as humans. We use God's mighty weapons, not worldly weapons to knock down strongholds of human reasoning, to destroy false arguments."

Today, in the name of Jesus Christ, I cast down the stronghold of human reasoning and mental calculations that limits me in life.

Henceforth, I put on the cloak of God's thinking.

And I command to be destroyed every false argument, every philosophy, every evil imagination, and every high thing that exalts itself against the knowledge of God in my mind.

I arrest every rebellious thought and declare them subject unto the obedience of Christ, in Jesus name.

I am created in the image of God.

I think like God and reason like Him.

I can never be frustrated.

I can never be stuck at one point.

As God can never be lonely and forsaken, so will I never be abandoned and forsaken because I have the creative power of the Almighty God, in Jesus name.

I decree and declare today that...

Through the wisdom of God, I will transform spiritual mysteries into global commodities.

I will create systems, influence systems, and upturn evil systems.

God empowers my mind to understand hidden secrets and heavenly protocols that turn things to my favor, in the name of Jesus Christ.

Even though I am an earthen vessel, God is molding me to His nature, every day.

I am housing divine treasures.

And every of God's invested treasure in me is being converted from potential to purpose, in the name of Jesus Christ.

Father, in the name of Jesus, I ask that every treasure, every talent, and every gift in my life be converted from potential to profit from today.

O Lord, send into my life people that will recognize the gifts and potentials you invested in me and help sharpen them for Your use, in Jesus name.

In the name of Jesus Christ, I receive the grace to become a millionaire.

May every false assumption in my mind concerning wealth be erased today.

My wealth will change the world for Jesus.

I declare in the name of Jesus that...

I am a compendium of grace, an embodiment of divine wisdom.

I carry the grace of God.

I am like Jesus. I do what he did.

I preach the Gospel, perform miracles in my place of work, heal the sick, and raise the dead.

As Jesus was never stranded, I will never be stranded.

Today, in the name of Jesus Christ...

I connect to the divine wisdom that will lead me to one hundredfold restoration.

I am having double for every trouble.

I will enjoy divine comforts, divine provisions, and divine abundance.

Thank You, Jesus, for answered prayers

PRAYER DAY 5: DIVINE IDEAS (1)

But thou shalt remember the Lord thy God: for it is he that giveth thee power to get wealth, that he may establish his covenant which he sware unto thy fathers, as it is this day. – Deut. 8:18

We are Abraham's children through Jesus Christ. So one of the reasons God wants to prosper us is to prove that we are indeed Abraham's children in Christ. Our prosperity establishes (confirms and fulfills)   God's covenant with our forefathers of the faith.

Poverty is an insult to the covenant. We cannot help the poor and broken world by being poor and broken as well. A poor man cannot help a poor man. You need means to make an impact around you. That is why it is essential to talk about financial breakthrough and wealth creation.

God said to Abraham, "I will bless you so that you will be a blessing to others." You can't be a blessing to others while under a curse yourself.

It is not right; in fact, it is evil for folly to be set in great dignity, while the rich sit in low places. It is wrong for fools to occupy high positions, while the wise walk barefooted. It is a spiritual error for servants and slaves to ride upon horses while princes walk as servants upon the earth (Ecc. 10:5-7). This is a grave foundational error that must be corrected.

Wealth creation is not all about money-making. It's more about correcting the foundational error being entrenched in the world by the evil systems of men. It's about validating the efficacy of the covenant and establishing the systems of God in our communities.

As God's children, we need means to stop the messes of the devil. By embracing God's mysteries and principles of wealth creation, we are not just talking about cash and savings. No. We are correcting the error in the world and entrenching a divine order.

So, how does God give us the power to create wealth?

DIVINE IDEAS

God's power to create wealth comes through ideas. These ideas, when pursued, does not only solve financial problems, they lead to the emergence of great businesses, products, solutions, books, songs, ministries, and the establishment of Godly systems. That's why we want to pray for divine ideas today.

When God gives you ideas, they do not only bring money; they also impact lives. They make others grow and want to know God, the more.

When we pray for money, God gives us ideas and leaves us with the choice to carry them out or not. God's ideas are the key to being fruitful, multiplying, replenishing the earth, and subduing it.

God's ideas usually see ahead; they may not make sense when we receive them, but they are the keys to unlocking the future.

Who would have ever thought that the principle of genetics that Jacob used to recover his stolen wages would eventually be developed by science? Today, it is possible to crossbreed animals because we have genetic science. It wasn't so in Jacob's time. Yet, he used a very similar strategy to breed animals with unique colors. No one taught him what it was then except God's Spirit. Imagine if he refused to try out the idea.

If you followed some of the ideas God gave to you many years ago, you wouldn't be where you are today. However, we bless God because there is grace for restoration. As we pray, God will renew and restore us.

HOW TO RECEIVE IDEAS FROM GOD

1. Recognize that you are creative by default and call forth your creative powers to action.

Elephants do not struggle to grow big; lions do not strive to become lions; birds do not struggle to fly. Why? Because by nature, they are created to be what their parents gave birth to them to be.

We are created in the nature and image of God. So we are co-creators by default. We are naturally creative. Creativity is in our genes. Our faculties are empowered to create and point others to a better way of doing things.

Call forth your creative nature by accepting that you have creative powers, and begin to prayerfully think of how to improve the dynamics of your job and business.

2. Don't make your focus about money only

As I said earlier, God's ideas are not just about money-making. Real kingdom prosperity is not about how much money we can make or grab here and there. Not at all. Money making is but the smallest aspect of the entire concept of kingdom wealth creation.

Kingdom prosperity and wealth creation is about establishing an order that enforces the system of God in the hearts of men. It's about bringing His kingdom on this earth as it is heaven.

Yes, we are praying for financial breakthrough; however, you must recognize that money is not the only instrument of financial breakthrough. In fact, ideas and direction are far more valuable than money.

So when you think about financial breakthrough, don't let your mind only go towards money. Focus more on value, solutions, products, ideas, and community help. Ask yourself:

- What value has God created me to add to my community?
- What problems can I solve for others?
- What difference can I make?
- What product can I bring to the marketplace?
- What special services can I render?
- What skills do I have that I can sell?

Note your answers and give yourself to working with the thoughts that God drops in your mind.

PRAYERS

Heavenly Father, I ask that Your Spirit will move in my heart and cause every darkness in my life to be removed in the name of Jesus Christ.

Every foundational error in my life causing lack, debts, poverty, and humiliation, may it be corrected from this day forward, in Jesus name.

Father, forgive me for every time I rejected Your idea in the past, either because of fear, or because of what people will say, or because of lack of acceptance.

Empower me to remember any idea You designed for me that is in Your package for my destiny, in the name of Jesus.

O Lord, connect me with men and women that will refire Your ideas in my life.

Help me to remember and recognize through chats, discussions, and observations the ideas that are from You, designed for me to entrench the realities of Your Kingdom on earth, in Jesus name.

I decree and declare today that…

I am creative by default

I make things happen

And I solve problems, in Jesus name

Holy Spirit, anoint my skill, anoint my business, and make the works of my hands to become a medium of global attention.

I declare today that I attract the right clients, the right customers, and the right corporate bodies to work with, in Jesus name.

Ephesians 2:10 - For we are his workmanship, created in Christ Jesus for good works, which God prepared beforehand, that we should walk in them.

......

I pray today, O Lord, may my business and career be aligned to divine purpose, in Jesus name

From today, I will not invest my time in projects, businesses, jobs, and opportunities that are not connected to God's agenda for my life, in the name of Jesus Christ.

Father, deliver me from shiny object syndrome; Cause me to focus only on the right opportunities that are divinely ordained to establish my financial freedom, in the name of Jesus Christ.

1 Kings 3:12 - "Behold, I give you a wise and discerning mind, so that none like you has been before you, and none like you shall arise after you."

•••••••

O Lord, give me a wise and discerning mind to recognize good and bad opportunities and help me to reject offers that are designed to destroy me or waste my resources, in Jesus name

---

Proverbs 22:29 - "Do you see a man skillful in his work? He will stand before kings; he will not stand before obscure men."

••••••••••

Father, baptize me with wisdom and the anointing to be skilled in my work.

Cause me to excel and be an example to others.

I declare that I will no longer labor and work in darkness.

My labor will be recognized and appreciated by kings and people that matter, in Jesus name

---

O Lord, weed out time-wasters and destiny destroyers from my life.

I declare that the work I do is unto the Lord.

Through my work and my business, God will be glorified, in Jesus name.

Thank You, Lord, for answered prayers.

From today, my mind is flowing with divine ideas that will command my financial dominion, in Jesus name.

"Call forth your creative nature by accepting that you have creative powers, and begin to prayerfully think of how to improve the strategies of your job and business.

PRAYER DAY 6: DIVINE IDEAS (2)

---

14 "Again, the Kingdom of Heaven can be illustrated by the story of a man going into another country, who called together his servants and loaned them money to invest for him while he was gone.

15 "He gave $5,000 to one, $2,000 to another, and $1,000 to the last—dividing it in proportion to their abilities—and then left on his trip. –

Matthew 25:14-15 (TLB)

No one needs to envy anyone in the kingdom. We are all gifted with money seeds designed to create our financial harvests. These money seeds are ideas.

As the scripture says, God has given us seeds according to our several abilities. So there is no need for envy and jealousy. Just recognize your own seeds and trade with them.

"Recognizing our money seeds is very important to command our financial dominion."

Yesterday, I shared two keys to discovering divine ideas designed to enforce your financial freedom. Let's see a few more insights that will help you uncover your power to create wealth.

3. LOOK AT PROBLEMS DIFFERENTLY

Sometimes, when we ask God for money, He shows us problems that are around us or the skills we have. I have learned that, sometimes, even in our pains are seeds of hope and prosperity.

If you prayerfully restudy the pains that God has led you through, maybe He is calling your attention to what you need to do for others, a problem you should solve. Something that when you start, it aligns you on the path of destiny and enforce His order on the earth.

Don't see problems as killers, but as opportunities in disguise. Yes, you may not understand them; you may not like them. No one does. But when you can, look beyond the pains and ask for the wisdom in it. They may contain the ideas you are looking for.

4. CRITICALLY LOOK AT YOUR HISTORY

Blessings and curses can be generational. Regrettably, we emphasize so much on generational curses without talking about generational blessings. Fortunately, generational blessings are a spiritual and Biblical reality.

The blessings of Abraham, which we access in Christ, is a generational blessing. Think about this: Abraham was a farmer. Isaac was a farmer. Jacob was a farmer. And even today, the Israelites still excel in farming.

Specific businesses, ideas, traits, or skills are inborn and built in a family line. That's why we need to look inwards and look through our history when praying for business and financial breakthrough. We need to ask ourselves, "are there skills, traits, solutions, or careers that our grandparents or parents were known for that we might have?" A critical look at the answer might expose some gifts and ideas that we have been ignoring.

Blessings are transferable; businesses, callings, ministries, and careers can move from a family generation to another generation because God does not see wealth as money to pay bills. He sees wealth as something generational. That's why the Bible says that a good man leaves an inheritance for his children's children (Proverbs 13:22). That inheritance is not only money; it also includes skillsets, ideas, and opportunities that can be developed, expanded, and traded with.

5. PRAY AND ASK GOD FOR AN IDEA.

Another way to receive business ideas is to pray and ask God for one. Every good and every perfect gift comes from God (James 1:17). If anyone lacks wisdom, he should ask from God, and He will give them (James 1:5).

6. THE MONEY SEED PRINCIPLE

Think of money as a seed, and find good grounds to plant them accordingly. In the parable of the talents above, the master gave them money and said, "use this money to trade."

You must recognize when the money in your hands is for trading, and not for something else. If you spend your trade and investment money on something else, you are wasting your seeds.

Don't eat your seeds. They are designed to be planted. That is, invested.

God always gives us seeds. Inside our seeds are forests if planted and nurtured. Unfortunately, many waste their seeds.

Henceforth, watch out for money seeds in your life, and prayerfully plant them for a better harvest.

If you don't recognize the seeds that God gives you, you may not experience the harvests He plans for you.

PRAYERS

Heavenly Father,

Open my eyes to discover the seeds of financial success that You bestowed on me.

Cause my heart, my imaginations, and all my faculties to recognize the ideas and resources I have received in Christ to trade with, resources designed to command influence in this world, and the heavens for Jesus, in Jesus name.

Father, deliver me from doubting Your gifts and skills in my life.

May every form of double-mindedness in me that empowers financial scarcity be destroyed today, in the name of Jesus Christ.

I declare today that...

I am no longer a doubleminded person.

I no longer doubt the gifts, skills, ideas, resources, and opportunities that God sends my way, in Jesus name

---

There is a seed in me to create my financial abundance.

As I pray and seek God, I will recognize these seeds and be empowered to plant and nurture them, in Jesus name.

I decree and declare today that I am like a tree planted by the riverside. I bear fruit in all seasons. I have no reason to be stranded.

When men are saying there's a casting down, the grace of God will be in me to keep saying, "Oh, there's a lifting up," in Jesus name.

From today, I receive the gift of the right people; I receive the gifts of helpers; I receive the gifts of people that will lift my hands in a time of need, in Jesus name.

Father, I pray that You will strengthen the works of my hands, and multiply my efforts, in the name of Jesus Christ.

Henceforth, everything will work together for my good;

My labor will produce abundance, and I shall excel financially, in Jesus name.

"Through wisdom, a house is built, and by understanding, it is established, and by knowledge, the rooms shall be filled with all precious and pleasant riches." - Proverbs 24:3-4

....

O Lord, give me the wisdom to build myself up in You. Give me the understanding to develop myself according to Your plans for my life. Give me the knowledge to establish myself in Your direction, and give me the anointing to attract precious and pleasant riches, in Jesus name.

I decree today that I have the knowledge to attract vast and lifelong riches.

I move away from scarcity, and I move into abundance.

As my doors open every day, and I step out of my house, as I go to work and invest in my business, I attract helpers; I attract clients, and I attract better offers, in the name of Jesus Christ.

Thank You, Lord Jesus Christ, for answered prayers.

Amen.

"God always gives us seeds. Inside our seeds are forests if planted and nurtured."

PRAYER DAY 7: NO MORE LIMITS

[28]*Have you not known? Have you not heard? The everlasting God, the Lord, the Creator of the ends of the earth, neither faints nor is weary. His understanding is unsearchable.*

[29]*He gives power to the weak, and to those who have no might He increases strength.*

[30]*Even the youths shall faint and be weary, and the young men shall utterly fall, [31]but those who wait on the Lord shall renew their strength; they shall mount up with wings like eagles, they shall run and not be*

weary, they shall walk and not faint. – Isaiah 40: 28-31

God is unlimited. His power is infinite, and there is nothing impossible with Him. It is we humans that put a cap on His ability. We put limitations on Him by thinking so poorly of Him.

The children of Israel tested God by not believing that He can take them through to the promised land. They defined boundaries on His power and sadly perished in the wilderness because of that.

If there's something that pains the heart of God, it is when we limit him. It is when we believe that God can do this, but cannot do that. Or when we think that, you know, this situation is too big.

Today, I want to speak to you as a prophet of God: take the limits off God. Increase your expectation.

Don't limit God to your debts. Don't limit Him to your mortgage. He can give you a house that you didn't build. Look unto Him and not your needs.

CREATE THE IMAGE OF ABUNDANCE

Your miracles are first created inside you before they manifest outside. What are the things that you believe inside you? It's time to enlarge your expectation. It's time to expand your thoughts.

Stop thinking, "Only if I can just get a hundred dollars to pay these debts, I'll be fine." Enlarge your expectation and believe for bigger miracles.

Stop looking at the mathematics of your age and wondering how the promises of God are going to happen. Release the limit and let God work in your life and finances.

> ***"Your abundance starts from within before it springs outside."***

God is speaking to you this today: "Stop limiting Me. Don't limit Me to your debts. Don't limit me to your rent. Don't limit Me to your children's school fees. I have something much bigger for you."

The Bible says in the book of Psalm 34:4, ***"I sought the Lord, and he delivered me from all my troubles, every one of them."***

God will deliver you from all your financial troubles, in Jesus name.

Let's do this: close your eyes for a few minutes and create an image of prosperity. Imagine yourself out of debts. Imagine yourself lending to others. Imagine yourself running a successful business. Imagine yourself in your own home. Imagine yourself donating thousands of dollars to charity and to different ministries.

Create a new image of success in your mind right now and listen to what God is saying in your heart about them. He says,

- "As you think in your heart, so are you."
- "It shall be unto you according to your faith."
- "Whatever I hear you say, that's what I will allow to happen to you."
- "Decree and declare that it may be well with you."
- "Arise and shine for your light has come."
- "You will rise again."

Declare the image in your spirit about yourself and about your finances.

It's time to stop hearing what your ex, your creditors, your lack and your bank balance is saying and stick with your new image and what God is saying.

Do you see yourself coming out of your debt?

Do you see yourself riding the waves of favor in your workplace?

Do you see yourself riding the waves of supernatural breakthroughs?

Do you see things turning around for your good?

Do you see yourself going from place to place as a blessing to others?

What do you see?

Whatever you see now, that's what is going to happen.

PRAYERS

Heavenly Father, I am sorry for putting a limit on You before now.

Today, O Lord, I take all limits off You.

I accept that You are interested in my financial wellbeing. You delight in my prosperity.

Thank You, Abba Father, in Jesus name.

In the name of Jesus Christ, I command every spirit of doubt and fear in me to leave.

I declare that I believe that it is well with me financially.

O Lord, I receive everything that is in Your plan for my life and destiny.

I am called to be a blessing.

Through me, people will be blessed.

I will go from place to place a blessing to others.

I will sow seeds here and there.

I will give here and there because God has empowered me to be a giver, in Jesus name

---

I decree and declare today that...

I receive grace and empowerment to be a millionaire in gold, silver, and bronze.

I receive grace, power, and strange supernatural intervention to be a millionare in dollars, pounds and other currencies of the world.

I eceive grace to be a lender to nations

My career and business receives grace and empowerment to excel.

I receive grace to prosper in my job beyond man's limits, in Jesus name.

Father, Lord, help me to trust You with my money always.

Help me to trust You to deliver me and set me on high for Your name's sake, in Jesus name.

In the name of Jesus Christ, I decree and declare that...

I have a flourishing ministry.

I have a global, flourishing career

I have a world-changing business

I am an employer of labor,

I declare today that...

I am rich in giving.

I am rich in mercy and kindness.

I am rich in power.

I am rich in love.

I am rich in forgiveness.

I am rich in health.

I am rich in money

I am rich in peace

I decree and declare that God has raised me to be a light that shines everywhere I am.

I am a light in my family.

I am a light in my home.

I am a light in my business.

I am a light in my ministry

I am a light in my office

O Lord, by Your power, reposition me for success.

Cause me to be at the right place and at the right time, in the name of Jesus Christ.

Thank You, Lord, for answering my prayers.

Thank You for causing me to have abundance in everything, in Jesus name.

Amen.

"Create a new image of success in your mind and listen to what God is saying in your heart about them."

GOD

BLESS

YOU

Get in Touch

We love testimonies.

We love to hear what God is doing around the world as people draw close to Him in prayer.

Please share your story with us.

Also, please consider giving this book a review on Amazon and checking out our other titles at:

amazon.com/author/danielokpara.

Kindly do check out our website at www.BetterLifeWorld.org, and send us your prayer request. As we join faith with you, God's power will be made manifest in your life.

OTHER BOOKS BY THE SAME AUTHOR

Latest Books

31 Days in the School of Faith

31 Days With the Heroes of Faith

31 Days With the Holy Spirit

31 Days With Jesus

31 Days in the Parables

None of These Diseases

I Will Arise and Shine

Psalm 91: His Secret Place, His Shadow, and His Protection

All Books

Prayer Retreat: 21 Days Devotional With Over 500 Prayers & Declarations to Destroy Stubborn Demonic Problems.

HEALING PRAYERS & CONFESSIONS

200 Violent Prayers for Deliverance, Healing, and Financial Breakthrough.

Hearing God's Voice in Painful Moments

Healing Prayers: Prophetic Prayers that Brings Healing

Healing WORDS: Daily Confessions & Declarations to Activate Your Healing.

Prayers That Break Curses and Spells and Release Favors and Breakthroughs.

120 Powerful Night Prayers That Will Change Your Life Forever.

How to Pray for Your Children Everyday

How to Pray for Your Family

Daily Prayer Guide

Make Him Respect You: 31 Very Important Relationship Intelligence for Women to Make their Men Respect them.

How to Cast Out Demons from Your Home, Office & Property

Praying Through the Book of Psalms

The Students' Prayer Book

How to Pray and Receive Financial Miracle

Powerful Prayers to Destroy Witchcraft Attacks.

Deliverance from Marine Spirits

Deliverance From Python Spirit

Anger Management God's Way

How God Speaks to You

Deliverance of the Mind

20 Commonly Asked Questions About Demons

Praying the Promises of God

When God Is Silent! What to Do When Prayer Seems Unanswered or Delayed

I SHALL NOT DIE: Prayers to Overcome the Spirit and Fear of Death.

Praise Warfare

Prayers to Find a Godly Spouse

How to Exercise Authority Over Sickness

Under His Shadow: Praying the Promises of God for Protection (Book 2).

Audio Books

120 Powerful Night Prayers that Will Change Your Life

28 Days of Praise Challenge: Dealing With Your Fears and Battles Through Intentional Praise

Anger Management God's Way: Bible Ways to Control Your Emotions, Get Healed of Hurts & Respond to Offenses ...Plus Powerful Daily Prayers to Overcome Bad Anger Permanently

<u>By His Stripes</u>: God's Promises & Prayers for Healing

<u>Deliverance of the mind</u>: Powerful Prayers to Deal With Mind Control, Fear, Anxiety, Depression, Anger and Other Negative Emotions.

<u>Healing Words: Daily Confessions & Declarations</u> to Activate Your Healing

<u>How God Speaks to You</u>: An ABC Guide to Hearing the Voice of God & Following His Direction for Your Life

<u>How to Exercise Authority Over Sickness</u>: Authoritative Prayers and Declarations for Personal Healing, and Healing of Your Loved Ones

<u>How to Meditate on God's Word</u>: Fast and Easy Ways to Practice Intentional Bible Meditation and Grow in Faith, Worship, and Prayer

<u>Prayers to Find a Godly Spouse</u>: Meditations, Prophetic Declarations and Biblical Foundation for Finding a Life Partner

<u>Praying the Promises of God</u> for Daily Blessings and Breakthrough

<u>Take it By Force:</u> 200 Violent Prayers for Deliverance, Healing and Financial Breakthrough

<u>Under His Shadow</u>: God's Promises and Prayers for Protection

<u>When God Is Silent</u>: What to Do When Prayers Seems Unanswered or Delayed

<u>Beside the Still Waters</u>: God's Promises and Prayers for Guidance and Direction | Learn to Know the Will of God & Make Right Decisions

<u>Less Panic More Hope</u>: God's Promises and Prayers to Overcome Fear, Anxiety, and Depression – Scriptures and Prayers for Mental Health

<u>How to Pray for Your Family</u>: Plus Over 70 Prayers for Your Family's Salvation, Healing, Restoration, and Breakthrough

<u>Prayers that Break Curses</u>: Everything You Need to Know About Curses, and Powerful Prayers to Stop All Kinds of Curses

<u>20 Commonly Asked Questions About Demons</u>: Answers You Need to Bind and Cast Out Demons, Heal the Sick, and Experience Breakthrough

<u>Deliverance by Fire:</u> 21 Days of Intensive Word Immersion, and Fire Prayers for Total Healing, Deliverance, Breakthrough, and Divine Intervention.

<u>Command Your Money:</u> Powerful Keys to Provoke Financial Breakthrough | 10 Simple Actions of Faith That Will Provoke Financial Breakthrough for Anyone in 30 Days or Less

NOTES